Colossians and Philemon

Take a New Look at Christ

Let the word of Christ dwell in you richly as you teach and admonish one another with all wisdom, and as you sing psalms, hymns and spiritual songs with gratitude in your hearts to God.

Colossians 3:16

CONCORDIA PUBLISHING HOUSE · SAINT LOUIS

Copyright © 1994 by Concordia Publishing House

3558 S. Jefferson Avenue

St. Louis, MO 63118-3968

1-800-325-3040 • www.cph.org

Edited by Rodney L. Rathmann

Manufactured in the United States of America

8 9 10 11 12 13 14   15 14 13 12

Contents

Leaders Notes

Lesson 1

Greetings from Paul
(Colossians 1:1–2)

Approaching This Study

Letters make up about one-third of the New Testament. They are important because they contain teachings of the apostles and their associates. The New Testament letters combine information about God and the Christian faith with instruction on life and behavior. In addition, they unpack some of the early church's problems and demonstrate how those problems were met. Take a few minutes to flip through the letters in your Bible—**Romans** through **Jude**. Which are the most familiar to you?

A fascinating thing about these New Testament books is that they *are* letters—not narratives, like the Gospels, not histories like the book of **Acts**, but letters—written under inspiration of the Holy Spirit by real people with real needs. It's helpful to keep this in mind as you listen to the epistle readings in church and, especially, as you begin this study of Paul's letters to the Colossian Christians and to Philemon. As you read, look for the personal elements in the letter: clues to the writer's personality and style of expression, references to the situation that prompted the letter and the way the writer deals with that situation, descriptions of the lives and personalities of the recipients, and hints about the relationship between the author and the readers. These elements will enrich the letters' message to you.

In Paul's world, letters were vital communication. There were no phones, no radios or televisions, no fax machines. The great distances and hazardous travel routes made frequent personal visits out of the question. So Paul had to rely on personal messengers to carry his written words to the far-flung congregations of the eastern Mediterranean. The letters were hand-written—often on papyrus, hand-delivered, and probably read aloud to groups of Christians. No doubt there was much eagerness and anticipation as listeners waited to hear the contents of the letter. There were probably interruptions for questions, discussion, clarification, and repetition of key sections.

An Overview

Unit Reading

Read the first two verses of Paul's letter to the Colossians. Choose one person to read these aloud to the group-preferably from a modem, easy to understand Bible translation. If you're doing the reading, try to put as much expression and feeling into the letter as you imagine the original readers might have done for the eager Colossian Christians.

The Message in Brief

In the writing style of the day, Paul begins his letter by naming himself as author and identifying his readers. In addition, Paul offers his credentials as an apostle and sends the Colossians greetings and a blessing. In these opening words you can already gather clues about Paul and his writing style. What purposes, other than identification, do these opening words serve? What is the purpose of the letter opening?

Working with the Text

Who Were the Colossians?

Colosse was a town in Phrygia, part of the Roman province of Asia, whose capital was Ephesus. It was situated in the beautiful Lycus River Valley and surrounded by mountains. As was the case with most Greek cities, Colosse was filled with diverse cultural and religious elements. Idolatry and paganism abounded. This, combined with the provincialism and pettiness of a city overshadowed by wealthier and more powerful neighbors, made it difficult for the Christian minority in Colosse. The temptation to stagnate or to compromise their witness to Christ was constant.

1. To better understand the situation Paul is addressing, a quick dip into sections of this and other letters is helpful. What conclusions about the social and cultural life of Colosse can you draw from **3:5–4:1**?

2. The Christian community in Colosse had been founded by a man named Epaphras, himself a Colossian (**1:7; 4:12**). Note how Paul addresses the congregation: he names them saints because the Holy Spirit had called them to faith in Jesus, to be a holy people of God. They are "faithful brethren" because they believed the Gospel. What spiritual blessings of these Christians does Paul mention in **1:12–14** and **2:13–14**? How would you explain those blessings to someone in your own church? To someone who is unfamiliar with Christianity?

Who Was Paul?

1. In **verse 1** Paul identifies himself as an apostle. What do you know about the apostle Paul? Describe him to one another. Once you've gotten past his background, concentrate on Paul, the man. What do you think he was like? How would you like to have him as your pastor? Your personal counselor? Your friend? How much of what you know is based on what you've heard from pastors and teachers, or from reading the historical accounts of his conversion and missionary journals? How much is based on what you've learned from reading his letters?

Paul had never been to Colosse. Most of the people who heard or read this letter had never met him. What difference might this have on Paul's writing style and tactics? To the Colossians' reception of the letter?

2. Paul was born in Tarsus in Asia Minor (**Acts 22:3**). He was a Jew (**2 Corinthians 11:22**), known before his conversion to Christ as Saul (**Acts 13:9**). He was of the tribe of Benjamin (**Philippians 3:5**) and was a committed Pharisee. At the same time, he enjoyed the privileged position of

Roman citizenship (**Acts 16:37ff**). Quickly review the account of Paul's conversion in **Acts 9:1–19**. How does this event explain Paul's conviction about his "call" in **Colossians 1:1** and **Galatians 1:1**?

Paul was imprisoned as a result of his vast and energetic missionary efforts. In **4:3, 10,** and **18,** he mentions his imprisonment. It is believed that Paul wrote this letter while in Rome, where he also wrote Ephesians and Philemon. If this epistle was indeed written from Rome, it can be dated AD 62 or 63. Paul had a ready-made opportunity to send the letter with Tychicus (who may also have carried the letter to the Ephesians at the same time) and Philemon's runaway slave Onesimus, whom Paul was sending home (see Lessons 12 and 13 on the letter to Philemon).

What Prompted the Letter?

1. The faith of the Colossian Christians was being threatened. Paul's letter was a response to, and ammunition against, those threats. Read **2:8** and **2:16–23**. What false notions does Paul warn against?

Some of the legalistic regulations were holdovers from Jewish converts who claimed that circumcision and dietary rules were necessary to Christianity and who insisted that Gentile Christians submit to ceremonial law.

A philosophy which posed a threat to early Christianity was known as Gnosticism. It held that what is spirit is good, while matter is inherently evil. If that were true, Christ would never have assumed a human form. To the Gnostics, Jesus only *seemed* to be human. He would not actually have taken a real, flesh-and-blood body, because flesh and blood are matter- and, as such, evil. And, to be free from such evil themselves, Christians must practice rigorous self-denial.

2. Why are Paul's warnings important? What might be the price of making Gentile Christians follow Old Testament ceremonial laws as a requirement for Christianity? What do **1:15–20** and **2:2–6** say to those who would confuse the person and work of Christ? Over and over, Paul had to remind Christians that salvation—membership in God's family—was a *gift,*

8

not something that could be earned by saying the right thing or by keeping certain rules and regulations.

What danger lurks if the Christian church forgets that salvation is a free gift from God?

A Quick Overview of the Letter

Colossians seems quite naturally to divide into five sections: the greeting, **1:1-2;** the person and work of Christ, **1:3–2:7;** the Christological and practical answer to heresy, **2:8–3:4;** encouragement to Christian living, **35–4:6;** personal news and notes, **4:7–18.** As you move through this Bible study, use the following columns to note relevant thoughts and words from Colossians that speak to the church today.

Location	Subject	Notes
1:1–2	**Greeting**	
1:3–2:7	**Christ's person and work**	
2:8–3:4	**Dealing with heresy**	
3:5–4:6	**Encouragement to Christian Living**	
4:7–18	**Personal Notes**	

Applying the Message

On the Larger Scene

1. How are Paul's warnings and affirmations still applicable today? Explain.

2. Is it still necessary to warn against error as strongly as Paul does? Why or why not? What should be our approach to those who are teaching error?

On a More Personal Level

1. If Paul were to write a letter to the Christian church today, what concerns might he address? What warnings or advice might he offer? For what would he praise and offer thanks?

2. Based on Paul's words in the first chapter of Colossians, how would you describe his attitude toward his readers? How might you reflect this kind of attitude in your relationship with others?

Taking the Lesson Home

Review

Read again Paul's greeting to the Christians in Colosse. This time, pause at the important words—*apostle, faithful, holy (saints), grace, peace*. Look up each word in a dictionary. Study the definitions carefully. Then read Paul's greeting again—slowly. Pause at each of the above words. Apply its meaning to yourself, your life. Try rewriting the greeting, capturing all the beauty and joy, but expressing Paul's thoughts in your own words.

Looking Ahead

Read the entire letter to the Colossians in one sitting. First put yourself in the role of one of the early Christians to whom Paul was writing. Then use the chart provided earlier in this lesson to make notes on how sections of the letter apply to today's church. Keep the notes handy as you meet and talk about Colossians in the coming weeks.

Working Ahead

Choose one or more of the following suggestions for further study. Make notes about your discoveries and bring these along to class in future lessons.

1. Examine a map of the New Testament world showing locations of Rome, where Paul wrote from prison, and Colosse and its surrounding towns and cities.

2. Browse through a dictionary, handbook, or encyclopedia of the Bible to learn more about Paul's letters, the congregation in Colosse, Paul's letter to the Colossians, and/or his life as a prisoner in Rome.

Lesson 2

Thankfulness and Prayer
(Colossians 1:3–14)

Approaching This Study

When we were children, we were taught to say "Thank you" whenever we received a gift or a favor. We expect a thank-you when we give gifts to others. We frequently close our letters with words of thanks. Giving thanks is a national custom; our government has designated a special holiday for thanksgiving. Unfortunately, like so many other "good manners" that we observe, thanksgiving often becomes an empty formality; its essence and meaning lost in the flurry of all our activities and cares.

Use the following survey to assess your experiences with thankfulness or thanksgiving. Check the statements that most honestly reflect your own attitude. Plan to briefly discuss your reactions with one another.

_____ 1. People who always seem cheerful and thankful are unrealistic and grate on my nerves.

_____ 2. Most of my prayers are of the "give me" or "help me" sort.

_____ 3. I begin each day with thoughts of thankfulness, finding something to look eagerly forward to.

_____ 4. I end each day thanking God.

_____ 5. I try to include words of thanks in every prayer, but even as I express these, nagging worries often drive the thanks out of my heart.

_____ 6. I am a thankful person.

_____ 7. I am a worrier.

_____ 8. I don't really understand thankfulness.

_____ 9. Thankfulness is a habit that can be learned.

_____ 10. I just don't ever seem to have time to feel thankful.

An Overview

Unit Reading

Read **Colossians 1:3–14.**

The Message in Brief

After his greeting, Paul begins on a positive note—words of thankfulness and encouragement. Why do you think Paul begins this way? What effect would his words have on the Colossian Christians?

Working with the Text

The Prayer of Thanksgiving (Colossians 1:3–8)

1. Look at Paul's thanksgiving and prayer in **1:3–5.** What is Paul thankful for, according to these verses? Why is this affirmation important for the Colossians to hear? Note the twofold thrust of the affirmation-the faith and love displayed by the Colossians. How did these two qualities work together in these Christians?

2. Now read **verses 6–8.** What is the source of the Colossians' faith? Why does Paul remind them of this source?

3. Paul himself apparently had not preached in Colosse; Epaphras brought the Gospel there (**1:7–8**). What do you learn about Epaphras in **verse 7**? What did Epaphras select as especially praiseworthy in the Colossian congregation (**v. 8**)?

Paul Prays for the Colossians (Colossians 1:9–11)

The Gospel motivates us to reflect God's love for us in Jesus. Note the transition words, "For this reason" ("And so"). *Because* of the good things he has heard about the Colossians, Paul continually prays for them. What does he ask God to do for them? Why does the thanksgiving lead into the request? Why is it important that the Colossians know about Paul's continual prayer? Why does it help you to know that people are praying for you? How does it help to know *what* they are praying for?

Paul's Reminder about Thanksgiving (Colossians 1:12–14)

1. Here Paul concludes this section—as he began it—with words of thankfulness. How would you summarize this reminder to the Colossians? Why is it so important that they give thanks?

2. What is the significance of the "light" and "darkness" images? In your own words, describe the "kingdom" to which the Colossians (and all Christians) belong. Include the ideas "light," "darkness," "redemption," and "forgiveness of sins" in your description.

Applying the Message

On the Larger Scene

1. Think about Paul's images of light and darkness to illustrate the Colossian Christians and the world in which they lived. Is this image equally appropriate for Christians in today's world? If so, do you see Christians shedding light in darkness? Can you cite evidence from world, national, or local news reports?

2. Paul's larger purpose in these beginning words of thanks and prayer is to affirm and strengthen the church at Colosse. On a purely secular level, this is just good psychology; you encourage the good qualities in people and they will continue to demonstrate those qualities. Think about the world in which you live and work. Do you see evidence of this kind of affirmation and encouragement in schools, businesses, neighborhoods, communities? How might Christians be instrumental in building such a spirit in their communities?

On a More Personal Level

1. Think again about the survey on thankfulness. How would you rate yourself on understanding, experiencing, and demonstrating genuine thankfulness? Try to pinpoint the reasons for your attitudes. Are these something you were born with? Did you learn them? From whom?

2. Now think about specific times when you've worked at feeling thankful. What are the most typical barriers to your experiences of gratitude? Try to list some of these.

3. Describe your understanding of a "thankful spirit." Where does it come from? How would it affect people's attitude toward themselves, their experiences, the world around them?

4. Do you think it's possible for a Christian to become a more genuinely thankful person? How might this happen? Here are a few idea starters. Check and then elaborate on any that you think might work for you.

___ Bible Study

___ Prayer

___ Christian friends

___ Devotional Topics

___ Receiving thanks from others

___ Discovering what others are thankful for

___ Expressing thanks to people around you

Taking the Lesson Home Review

Read again Paul's words of thankfulness and prayer. Read them slowly and carefully. Think of these words as part of a letter to you, from your church leader. (In a very real sense, this is true.) Sense the warmth of knowing that others are vocally thankful for *you*, for your faith and for the love you demonstrate to others. Then offer a prayer of thanksgiving for special Christians whom you know.

Looking Ahead

In **Colossians 1:15–23** Paul begins to tackle some of the problems facing the Colossian church. He approaches this task skillfully by reviewing what the Colossians may already know about Christ and by building on this knowledge. Read this section of the letter before the next session. Note the solid basis of understanding that Paul builds and compare this with your own understanding of the person and work of Jesus.

Working Ahead

Select one or more of these topics for additional study. Be prepared to report your findings at the next session.

1. Continue your notebook on the apostle Paul. Add discoveries from the text covered in today's lesson.

2. Leaf through the section of a hymnbook devoted to praise, thanksgiving, or worship. Select a hymn that is especially meaningful to you and study its words. Bring it along to the next session to use as a class prayer. If you're willing to do so, talk with the class about why you find the hymn's words so meaningful.

3. Read **Philippians 4:4–9**—part of another letter Paul wrote to a struggling group of early Christians. Think about how these words relate to your discussions about thankfulness and thanksgiving.

4. If you don't already do so, begin a daily exercise of thanksgiving. Choose a time and place where you can be alone and quiet with your thoughts. To help yourself focus, start by listing in a notebook events from that day. Leave several lines between each item on your list. After you've completed the list, use the lines below each event to write thoughts and feelings that might help you focus on how God's presence, love, and forgiveness can turn or has turned each into a blessing. Add to the notebook each day throughout this course. At the end of the course, share any results of this activity.

Lesson 3

A Picture of Christ (Colossians 1:15–23)

Approaching This Study

No thinking person joins a club or organization without first knowing some basics about it: what it stands for, how and why it was started, what it does. In most organizations, it is the leader or founder who sets the tone and defines the identity. Often, there are training sessions and briefings in which new members get to meet the founder or study materials describing the founder(s)—their background, how and why they started the group.

In no other group is the founder so important as in the Christian church. In no other group is it so essential to know the founder. Many Christians echo this conviction when they talk about "knowing Jesus as my Lord and Savior" as they confess their faith. This sort of *personal* knowledge is extremely important. However, we need to build such a relationship on a clear understanding of who Christ is and what He has done for us.

What do you know about Jesus? Take a few minutes to pool your knowledge with members of a small group. Use the space below to list some essentials about Christ-things that you might share with new believers or potential Christians. Remember, this is information about who Christ is and what He has done. Draw on what you have been taught in church and Sunday school, what you have discovered from parents, friends, personal Bible study, etc. When you have completed and discussed the list with the class, you will explore Paul's description of Christ in the letter to the Colossians.

An Overview

Unit Reading

Again read **Colossians 1:15–23** aloud—as it might have been read to the early Christians.

The Message in Brief

Recall the situation that had prompted this letter from Paul—the Colossians' faith was being threatened by false teachings. One of those heresies involved confused notions about the person and work of Jesus Christ. Paul had prepared his readers with a warm greeting and words of encouragement and prayer. It was now time for him to address some of the weightier issues on his mind.

How does this section of the letter compare with what came before it? How would you describe the tone of these paragraphs?

Working with the Text

The Christ Hymn (Colossians 1:15–20)

1. This portion of the letter is often called "the Christ-hymn." In what ways is it hymnlike? How do these verses compare to hymns that Christians sing today? If you were to include it in your own hymnal, which section might it come under? Why would these verses be important to the early Christians?

2. *Christ is the Image of God.* In **verses 15–17** and **19,** Paul speaks of Christ as "the image of the invisible God." Recall from the Genesis account of creation that God made man in His own image. However, when man sinned, he clouded and distorted that image. Christ has been described as a "second Adam." In what sense is this true? Study these verses and **verse 2:9.** What do they tell you about "the image of God"? Paul also states that Christ was present and active in the creation of heaven and earth. What truth about Jesus is clearly affirmed in these verses?

3. *Christ is head of the church.* **Verse 18** describes Christ's relation- ship to the church. Why do you think Paul chose this image? Expanding on such an image, how would you describe your role in the church?

4. *Christ is the firstborn from the dead* (**verse 18**). In ancient Israel, the firstborn was given a special right of place and privileges. What is the significance of Christ being called "firstborn from among the dead"? What promise does such a description hold for you and all Christians?

5. *Christ is the great unifier.* The Living Bible paraphrases **verse 20,** "It was through what His Son did that God cleared a path for everything to come to Him—all things in heaven and on earth—for Christ's death on the cross has made peace with God for all by His blood." Another word for "uniting" or "bringing together" is *reconciling.* In what sense is Christ "the great uniter" or reconciler? How does He reconcile you to God? What does this mean to you and to your life?

Reconciliation (Colossians 1:21–22)

1. In these verses, Paul expands on the concept of reconciliation, applying it to the Colossian Christians and to all who believe in Christ. What had previously separated the Colossians from God? How had Christ changed this? What effect did Christ's work have on the Colossians and on their relationship with God?

2. Look at the images Paul uses in the second part of **verse 22**: "to present you holy in His sight, without blemish and free from accusation." The words "without blemish" were used to describe animals that were considered suitable for sacrifice. Why would Paul describe reconciled Christians in this way? How is it that we remain holy and without blemish even though we continue to sin?

A Cautionary Note (Colossians 1:23a)

Paul attaches a brief caution or provision to the great news about reconciliation: "*if* . . ." Express this cautionary note in your own words. Why do the Colossian Christians—and *all* Christians—need this reminder? Is this meant to serve as a kind of club, to inspire fear in Christians? Explain why Paul felt it necessary to add such a reminder. Is this something you need to hear as well?

A Personal Note from Paul (Colossians 1:23b)

Note Paul's elaboration on "the Gospel" and mention of his own role in proclaiming that Gospel. Why did he point out that this was "the gospel that you heard and that has been proclaimed to every creature under heaven"? Why the emphasis on his own relationship to that Gospel—"of which I, Paul, have become a servant"?

Applying the Message

On the Larger Scene

1. Some Christians sneer at what they call "intellectual knowledge" about Jesus—His person and work. The important thing, they say, is to know and accept Jesus as "Lord and Savior"—to have a close, personal relationship with Him. How would you respond to this attitude?

2. Confusion about the person and work of Jesus has always plagued the church. It is important that Christians understand clearly Jesus' divine *and* human nature. How might too much emphasis on His human or divine nature affect our attitude about Christ's work? About salvation? About life here on earth? About our relationships with one another?

On a More Personal Level

1. Think about Paul's pictures of Christ in the letter to the Colossians—the image of God, the head of the church, the firstborn from the dead, the great uniter. Which picture do you find most personally appealing and meaningful? Explain.

2. Look again at the description of Christ you composed early in the session. How does it compare with the one provided by Paul? Which of your notes—if any—would you add to Paul's words to the Colossians?

3. Write another brief description of the person and work of Jesus Christ. This time, make it a personal sketch, based on what you have learned and your relationship with Him.

How does this description compare with the one you made earlier?

Taking the Lesson Home

Review

Read again **Colossians 1:15–20**. Think about the beauty and grandeur of these words and descriptions. Consider memorizing these verses as a personal or family creed for use in home devotions or Bible studies.

Looking Ahead

In **Colossians 1:24–2:5** Paul inserts a personal note about his own calling and ministry. Read these verses before the next session. Notice how Paul uses them as a transition in his letter. See what you can discover about Paul, the man, as you listen to him talk about his work.

Working Ahead

Select one or more of these suggestions for additional study in preparation for future sessions in this course.

1. Look up entries for "Christ" in a Bible dictionary, handbook, or encyclopedia. Compare the information you find with Paul's description of Christ and with the two descriptions you wrote in class.

2. Continue your notebook about Paul. You should be able to add some interesting insights about Paul from the readings in this session and the next.

Lesson 4

Job Description—Minister, Servant of the Gospel (Colossians 1:24–2:5)

Approaching This Study

Perhaps the most consistent, and seemingly incongruous, refrains in Paul's writing are his expressions of joy and thankfulness in his ministry on the one hand, and the tremendous suffering he experiences because of the Gospel on the other. If you read his letters carefully, you can't fail to see the flesh and bones of this great church leader. Paul seemed compelled to share his triumphs and failures, his confidence and insecurity in every letter he wrote.

This section of his letter to the Colossians contains revealing insights about the experiences and responsibilities of all whom God has called to faith in Christ Jesus. It also reveals much about Paul himself. What are your responsibilities as a Christian? Rank these from most important to least important.

An Overview

Unit Reading

Read **Colossians 1:24–2:5** silently. As you read, underline any words or phrases that describe Paul's role as minister; circle any words or phrases that apply to all Christians.

The Message in Brief

Paul tells the Colossians that his work for them has cost him suffering. He speaks of the wonderful truth God has revealed to them—the mystery of God's love in Christ—which Paul has been privileged to share with them and other non-Jews. Then he talks about the scope and purpose of his ministry, and attributes his great energy in this task to the power Christ gives him. Finally, Paul again reminds the Colossians of how much he has prayed for them and for the church at Laodicea, encourages them to grow in love and faith, and praises them for their firm faith and their loving relationships with each other.

Working with the Text
Paul's Ministry of Suffering (Colossians 1:24)

1. Paul begins this section of the letter with a rather startling claim—he finds great joy in his ministry even though it has brought him sufferings. Look at **verse 24**. What kind of suffering might result from Paul's ministry?

2. How might Paul find genuine joy in suffering for the Gospel?

Paul's Ministry of the Word (Colossians 1:25–2:1)

1. These verses contain a beautiful description of Paul's ministry. Paul again refers to the commission he received from God (discussed in Lesson 1) and explains that commission as "to present to you the word of God in its fullness." Then he describes the Gospel as a "mystery that has been kept hidden for ages and generations." How does Paul define the "glorious riches

of this mystery"? In what sense is the Gospel a mystery? What effect might Paul's choice of words have on the Colossians?

2. Paul refers to his work as labor and a struggle. Where does the power to struggle come from? How do these verses make you feel about Paul as a leader and as a man? What do the verses say to pastors, church leaders, and lay people today?

The Point of the Struggle (Colossians 2:2–5)

Paul explains the threefold purpose of his work as a minister of the Gospel: to lead God's people to a proper understanding of the mysteries of Christ, to help them escape from error, and to bring them stability of faith. How are all three of these really aspects of the same goal?

Applying the Message

On the Larger Scene

1. What obligations do Christian ministers have to the people they serve? to the Lord whom they serve?

2. What obligations do Christian lay people have to their pastor? to their congregation?

On a More Personal Level

1. Think again about Paul's words regarding the suffering that accompanied his ministry. Is this something unique to Paul, or do you expect the same kind of suffering in your own life as a Christian? Have you experienced any suffering for the Gospel? Do you, like Paul, find joy in such suffering?

2. How might suffering be transformed into a blessing—for Paul, for a pastor, for any Christian? Remember, the question is not "How might suffering be a blessing?" but "How might suffering be *transformed* into a blessing?"

3. Describe the partnership of pastor and people in the ministry of the congregation. How important is this partnership?

Taking the Lesson Home

Review

Read again Paul's words about his own ministry. Think about those words in terms of relationships and responsibilities within your church—your pastor, elected leaders, and lay people—and in terms of your own role in the congregation. Focus on the strengths of the relationships. Pray about these for guidance when weaknesses surface. Pray for your leaders.

Looking Ahead

In **Colossians 2:6–15** Paul addresses some of the threats facing these early Christians and advises them to cling to the truth they have learned about Christ. Read these words of advice prior to the next class session and begin to apply them to your own life.

Working Ahead

Select several of the following suggestions for additional study at home.

1. Look up "suffering" in a Bible concordance and read other biblical passages that speak about its cause, ways to endure it, and the potential for growth through suffering.

2. Find out more about your pastor—personal things such as interests, hobbies, family, etc. Include what you learn in your prayers for him. Write him a letter in which you express gratitude for the gifts of leadership he has shown to the church.

3. Consult a Bible dictionary or encyclopedia and a church history book to discover more about the role of pastors and leaders and church government among the early Christians.

Lesson 5

Putting Down Roots
(Colossians2:6–15)

Approaching This Study

This section of Colossians contains perhaps one of the most beautiful passages in the letter—full of warmth, wisdom, and helpful advice. In these verses, Paul urges the new Christians to sink their roots deep in Christ and continue to grow in Him.

Think about the image of roots in terms of your own life. Where have you "put down roots"? List some of your roots in the space below: your house and home, your family and friends, your job, schools, community, clubs or organizations, the church. After each item, describe how you have put down roots in each. Then briefly describe the kind of stability and nourishment each provides you. Keep this list in mind as you later discuss Paul's advice about roots.

1.

2.

3.

4.

An Overview

Unit Reading

Read **Colossians 2:6–15** by paragraphs (**vv. 6–7; 8; 9–12; 13–15**). Note how this encouragement to faithfulness is closely tied to Paul's description of his apostolic ministry.

The Message in Brief

The purpose of Paul's apostolic ministry was to lead God's people to a greater understanding of the good news of their redemption through Jesus Christ. Paul speaks of this message as "the word of truth, the Gospel" **(15)**. This knowledge of God's mystery **(2:2)** was to help the believers at Colosse to escape from spiritual delusion and bring them stability of faith **(2:5)**. Christians who are rooted in the apostolic Gospel are better equipped to distinguish sound teaching from false teaching. In this section of his letter, Paul warns his readers to beware of philosophy and empty deceit. He encourages them once again to persevere in the teaching they have received.

Working with the Text

Rooted in Christ (Colossians 2:6–7)

1. Believers confessed Christ Jesus as Lord. Note that the name *Jesus* means "Savior." Read **Matthew 1:21** for the significance of His personal name. *Christ* means "the anointed one," the Messiah. As Messiah and Savior, Jesus is also the Lord. What does this confession tell us about the person and work of Jesus? What do we know about the people who by faith confess, "Jesus Christ is Lord?

2. Paul urges the Colossians to continue living in Christ, "rooted and built up in Him." How can a Christian be "rooted and built up" in Christ? What does God's promise to sustain us and Paul's prayer to keep us "rooted in Christ mean for the times when we struggle with doubt and temptation?

Empty and Deceptive Philosophy (Colossians 2:8–9)

1. Here is another warning about temptations that may lead the Colossians away from the faith they had been taught. Paul uses a rather unusual image in this warning: "See to it that no one *takes you captive* through hollow and deceptive philosophy." How is this an appropriate image for temptation? Who seeks to take God's people captive?

2. In Paul's day the word "philosophy" (love of wisdom) described various teachings. Among the Greeks, philosophy was generally understood as knowledge of divine mysteries and wisdom. Note Paul's reference to this in **2:3**. Philosophical teaching was also known as a tradition. "The basic principles of this world" often referred to ruling spirits and signs of the zodiac. Recall what you learned in lesson 1about the Christian minority in Colosse. Why was Paul worried about the temptations facing the Colossian Christians?

3. In **verse 9** Paul repeats an affirmation he had made earlier (**1:19**): "In Christ all the fullness of the Deity lives in bodily form." Why do you think he felt compelled to repeat this at this point in the letter?

Alive in Christ (Colossians 2:10–15)

1. Note the beautiful transition—in *Christ* is the fullness of God; *you* have been given fullness in Christ. What is Paul saying about the believers in Colosse and the gift that is theirs? Recall that Paul had just written about the "hollow and deceptive philosophy" that surrounded and tempted the Colossians. "Don't be fooled by that, when you can have so much more," he says in the following verse. How would you describe the "fullness" that Christ offers?

2. In **verses 11–13** Paul uses another image to describe the Christians' new status under the Gospel: "In Him you were also circumcised . . . with the circumcision done by Christ." Read about circumcision as instituted in **Genesis 17:9–14**. Circumcision was an outward sign of God's people, of commitment and dedication to God. What does the "circumcision done by Christ" signify?

3. In the final two verses of this section, Paul dwells on the forgiveness that Christ won by His death for our sins. In what sense do we "die" with Christ and rise, with Him, to new life? What does this death and resurrection

imagery have to do with Paul's earlier description of the fullness of life that is ours in Christ?

Applying the Message

On the Larger Scene

What competing philosophies of life vie for our attention in America today? How do they try to appeal to the human desire for roots and stability?

On a More Personal Level

1. Think about Paul's encouragement to be "rooted and built up in" Christ. How can you—and all Christians—sink your roots deep in Christ? List as many ways as you can think of.

2. How do such roots offer stability to the Christian in day-to-day life?

3. Paul made a rather large point of the fullness of life that comes when Christians are rooted in Christ. Think carefully about the enormity of this promise: Christ gives us a life that is *full*. Describe fullness of life from your own experience as a Christian.

Taking the Lesson Home

Review

Read again **Colossians 2:6–15** in a quiet moment at home. Read the words aloud. Think about your efforts to be rooted and grow in Christ. Name ways in which your life is richer, fuller, because of God's gift of faith. Pray for continued growth and fullness in your life.

Looking Ahead

Read **Colossians 2:16–23**. Paul has warned the Colossian Christians against hollow philosophies and assured them of the fullness of life in Christ. Now he compares the slavery that results from following those philosophies with the wonderful freedom that we are given in Christ.

Working Ahead

Select one or more of the following topics for additional study.

1. Continue to add discoveries and insights to your notebook on Paul. You might want to include a section devoted to the images he uses to teach Christians about faith and life in Christ.

2. Talk with friends or family members about "putting down roots." Listen to their attitudes about "roots" and stability in life. What do these people seem to want from the roots they develop? Compare these to that which Christianity offers?

3. Advertisements and commercials contain some of the most powerful and effective examples of current philosophies of life. The people who create these ads have a remarkable understanding of the needs and wants of our society. Study some of these ads and commercials carefully. What needs do they appeal to? Note the empty, materialistic way in which they promise to meet those needs. Can you learn anything from these ads about a more effective way to present the Christian faith—the only true answer to such needs?

Lesson 6

Shadow and Reality, Slavery and Freedom (Colossians 2:16–23)

Approaching This Study

What does it mean to be a Christian? This, in essence, is the question that Paul addresses in all of his letters to the early church. In Paul's time, as in our own, confusion and disagreement arose among Christians over what was and was not essential to the faith. Each congregation faced unique challenges and threats. In his writing, Paul very carefully addresses these, one-by-one, pointing out the underlying errors and countering each with the truth of Christ's Gospel. The purpose of Paul's letters was to educate—to equip—the churches, so they could assess for themselves any future questions or challenges (which would certainly arise) in the light of Christ and the Gospel.

An Overview

Unit Reading

Read **Colossians 2:13–23** aloud. The first three verses were covered during the previous session, but notice how they provide a lead-in to today's material (**2:16–23**)—the transitional "therefore" serves as a bridge between thoughts.

The Message in Brief

Paul had warned the Colossian Christians against "hollow and deceptive philosophy, which depends on human tradition and the basic principles of this world rather than on Christ." He also reminded his readers that they share the fullness of Christ; victory over powers, principalities, spirits, and

38

elements of the universe has been gained by the cross of Christ. Through faith, the Christian shares Christ's victory over sin, death, and the power of evil. Paul now points out that believers in Christ are "therefore" free from the elements, rules, and regulations which would restrict their full freedom in Christ Jesus. Salvation has been won for them. Therefore, Christians are not bound to rules such as what to eat or drink or which holidays to observe. Such Old Testament practices are no more than a shadow of the reality—which is Christ. We depend on Him, not on ourselves, our spirituality, or self-imposed worship.

Working with the Text

Legalism and Slavery (Colossians 2:16–19)

1. In the old covenant God's people were bound to many ceremonial and dietary rules. **Leviticus 11** relates various food regulations. **Leviticus 23** speaks of feasts and festivals. What was the purpose of these rules and regulations? What does Paul call them in **Colossians 2:17**? Were they meant to be permanent rules for the spiritual life of God's people? How did Christ's life and work affect such rules and regulations?

2. In addition to excessive concern about foods and festivals, some within the Colossian congregation also advocated self-abasement or asceticism—an extreme form of self-denial. What does Paul mean by accusing these persons of being "puffed up"? In what sense are all who trust in their own reason or actions "puffed up"?

3. Paul speaks about "shadows" and "reality." Shadows are made by something real—a body, for example. Explain how Old Testament regulations were the shadow of what was to come, and Christ was the reality. How does Christ's existence affect His followers' attitude toward

and adherence to these rules and regulations? Would it be acceptable for these Christians to continue observing rules and regulations or some forms of self-denial? Explain.

Freedom in Christ (Colossians 2:20–23)

1. Paul has already reminded the Colossians that they were buried with Christ in their baptism and raised with Christ through their faith in Him. In what sense are these Christians "dead" to the world? What does this say about loving and living for any of the things of this world? How is the Christian's new life a freedom from slavery?

2. What, according to **verses 21–22**, were some of the taboos people tried to impose on Christians? Can you think of similar "taboos" fostered by some today? What is so dangerous about imposing these requirements on people?

3. In **verse 23** the apostle writes that regulations such as those mentioned above "have an appearance of wisdom, with their self-imposed worship, their false humility and their harsh treatment of the body." In what sense might adherence to such rules seem "wise"? Explain what Paul means by saying that these rules "lack any value in restraining sensual indulgence."

Applying the Message

On the Larger Scene

1. Paul frequently cautions the Colossian Christians not to slip back into bondage or slavery. What forms of slavery attract Christians today?

2. From time to time, newspapers carry stories about so-called "Christian" cults whose members meet unspeakably tragic fates. We are often stunned when we read about the rules, rituals, restrictions, and demands such cults make on their members. And yet similar cults continue to spring up and thrive today. What is their appeal? Why are people so willing—even eager—to give up everything and submit themselves to rigorous self-denial and self-abuse in order to belong?

3. What dangers await Christians who submit to legalistic rules and regulations?

On a More Personal Level

1. What does it mean to you and for your life to say that because we are servants of Jesus Christ we are truly free?

2. Why is freedom in Christ an especially difficult concept to understand and practice?

3. This portion of Colossians indicates that Christians have considerable freedom of expression in matters of religious practices (worship, custom, festivals, etc.). According to **1 Corinthians 14:40** and **1 Corinthians 9:19–23**, what limits or directs that freedom? How might such limits show themselves in our religious life?

Taking the Lesson Home

Review

Think carefully about the main points of today's lesson: Because Christ has fulfilled the law perfectly, we are freed from slavery to the law; because He suffered punishment for all the times when we disobey God's law, we are forgiven—we are free. With this gift of freedom comes Christ's power to direct our lives toward fullness and true joy. Offer a prayer of thanks for this freedom and a prayer for strength to follow Christ's direction in your life.

Looking Ahead

Read **Colossians 3:1–11**, where Paul begins to explain what this newness in Christ means to the daily lives and deeds of Christians.

Working Ahead

Choose one or more of the following suggestions for supplementary work.

1. Think about the expression "Christians live *in* the world, but they are not *of* the world." How does this expression describe what Paul wrote in today's section of Colossians? What does such a statement say to your own life and struggles with priorities?

2. Continue adding to your notebook on Paul.

Lesson 7

New Life—What It Is Not
(Colossians 3:1–11)

Approaching This Study

This session is all about changed people and changed lives. Before launching into the biblical material, take a quick personal survey. Be as honest as possible. Your answers are for your eyes only.

If I could change two things about myself, I would be
1. Less . . .   and more . . .

2. Less . . .   and more . . .

How difficult was it to come up with two changes?

When have you had such thoughts?

Why would you like to make those changes?

From your own experience, are such changes likely?

An Overview

Unit Reading

Read **Colossians 3:1–11**. In this section of his letter, Paul writes about changes. Again, notice how Paul begins by first laying a firm foundation for what will follow, "Since, then, you have been raised with Christ. . . ." As you read, try to form a picture of the Colossians' former life—the sort of life that Paul is urging them to give up.

The Message in Brief

The first part of Paul's letter to the Colossians has been doctrinal or instructional. Paul has especially stressed the universal lordship of Jesus. He now turns to the theme of sanctification—the Christian life. The apostle challenges God's people to demonstrate their faith in Jesus Christ by the way they think, the things they say, the way they act toward one another—in short, by their very lives. He begins the section with another reminder that the Christian has been raised from spiritual death to spiritual life.

Working with the Text

Motive and Power for Change (Colossians 3:1–4)

1. Paul begins his description of the new life in Christ—the change—with another reminder, "you have been raised with Christ." What does he mean by those words? Explain how they apply to all Christians—yourself included.

2. What comfort and power come from knowledge that Christ is now "seated at the right hand of God"? How does this knowledge enable Christians to set their minds on things above?

3. Think about the common encouragement to "set your sights higher." What does this expression mean to Christians? What is the final outcome or result of such "high sights" for the Christian? What will they ultimately see?

Killing the "Old Life" (Colossians 3:5–9)

1. Remember Paul builds upon what he has already written. Carefully review **2:11–13**. What does Paul mean by the "old life" or "earthly nature"? What must be done with it?

2. Paul first describes the Christian life by saying what it is *not*—what it is to be "put to death." In your own words, list those things which are to be absent from the Christian's life.

3. Why is it necessary for Paul to mention these sins to people who have heard the Gospel and have declared their faith in Christ?

4. Read **verse 6** and compare it with **Romans 1:18–20**. What is God's attitude toward sin? Does this attitude apply to Christians? Why or why not?

46

Taking on the New Life (Colossians 3:10–11)

1. Explain what Paul means by comparing the "new life" in Christ with putting on "the image of its Creator." (Think about the earlier discussion of God's image—the image that Adam originally bore, and that Christ demonstrated perfectly.)

2. In **verse 11** Paul begins to describe the evidences of this new life—in this case, as it is reflected in relationships among Christians. Explain what Paul means that "there is no Greek or Jew, circumcised or uncircumcised, barbarian, Scythian, slave or free." How is this relationship explained by the words "Christ is all, and is in all"?

Applying the Message

On the Larger Scene

1. Think about the list of sins which Paul describes as being part of the "old life." Which of these might bear mentioning to Christians today? Can you think of others that might be added?

2. How much "evidence" of faith is necessary in the life of a Christian? Is the evidence the same for all? What does this say about our tendency to judge others? What approach might you take with a friend who claims to be a Christian but shows no evidence of faith in her/his life?

3. Think again about the opening discussion regarding change and people's desire to change themselves. On the basis of your understanding of Christianity, how would you explain this universal longing? What is at its root?

4. There has been considerable debate and disagreement among psychologists and psychiatrists about whether it is, in fact, possible for adults to change—at least in any major way. How would you respond to this issue?

On a More Personal Level

1. All change requires death and rebirth. Probably the biggest obstacle to change is an unwillingness to "kill off" or give up our sinful ways. Think about your own experiences as a Christian. Why is it so difficult to put the old life to death? What experiences or assurances may help the process along?

2. Often, Christians are tempted to rationalize their failure to put to death the old life: "God is kind and loving. He doesn't really punish sin." Or "It doesn't really matter if I sin, since God has promised to forgive me." Or they think they can hang onto some of their old sinful ways (a sort of "security blanket"), believing that they will give them up and get them forgiven later-in plenty of time for any kind of judgment. How common do you think such attitudes are? How would you respond to these attitudes?

Taking the Lesson Home

Review

Review this week's section of the letter, listing sins that Paul urges the Colossian Christians to "put to death." Which of those sins are still alive and well in your own life? Concentrate on one or two that you find most difficult to leave behind. Pray about them. Experience Christ's forgiveness wipe these away. Ask for His power to put them out of your life. Make this prayer and renewal a daily effort.

Looking Ahead

Read **Colossians 3:12–17**, where Paul lays out a beautiful description of the new life in Christ and explains how this new life shows itself in words and actions.

Working Ahead

Choose one or more of the following suggestions for individual work.

1. Reread the portions of Paul's letter to the Colossians that have been covered thus far. Approach it as a letter addressed specifically to you or your family. Read it aloud—either to yourself or to other family members. Try to incorporate everything you've studied and discussed thus far into the reading. Which sections speak most powerfully to you? Circle these in your Bible and use them as the basis for daily meditations during the coming days and weeks.

2. List some of the problem areas in your own efforts to live a new life-sins that you have trouble putting to death. Behind each, write a brief prayer asking for God's power to leave these behind. Then list a quality of the new life in Christ (see **Colossians 3:12–17** for ideas) that could replace each sin. Ask for God's help in bringing about these transformations.

3. Study **Colossians 3:11**. This verse describes the relationships of love and equality that mark the new life in Christ. Rewrite this verse to apply to classes, groups, and attitudes in your life.

4. Continue adding to your notebook on Paul. What do this week's verses reveal about Paul's understanding of the Gospel? of the human condition? What might the understandings revealed in these verses indicate about Paul's own struggles?

Lesson 8

New Life—What It Is
(Colossians 3:12–17)

Approaching This Study

In the previous session, we explored what the Christian life is *not*. Now it's time to examine what it *is*. In this portion of his letter to the Colossian Christians, Paul goes into some detail about marks or features of Christian living. Before exploring Paul's thoughts, however, take a few minutes to share with one another your ideas about characteristics that demonstrate Christian faith. List your ideas in the space below:

Five Characteristics That Will Result from Faith in Christ

1.

2.

3.

4.

5.

An Overview

Unit Reading

Read **Colossians 3:12–17.** Paul urges the Colossian Christians to "set your mind on things above." At the same time, they are to put to death what is "earthly" in them. In addition to sexual excesses and covetousness, they are to put away anger and foul talk. They must not lie to each other. In brief, they are to put off the old nature and keep putting on the new. Paul reminds them that in their baptism, they died to sin and were raised with Christ to new life. As new people in Christ, they are to demonstrate the Christian life. Now Paul begins to describe that new life. His advice is simple, yet pointed—here is how Christians should live with one another.

The Message in Brief

Notice the beautiful, loving, way in which Paul prefaces his appeal: "Therefore, as God's chosen people, holy and dearly loved. . . ." After this reminder, Paul expresses the kind of behavior that must naturally demonstrate itself in the lives of these Christians: forgiveness toward one another—demonstrated in compassion, kindness, humility, gentleness, patience; a spirit of love and peace; and communal worship and thanksgiving to God. This kind of life involves a resolve to become more like Christ, to take on His character. Christ's life—His love and forgiveness—motivates us. His word shapes our thinking. The hallmark of Christian living is prayer and thanksgiving, and unselfish love to others. Our concern is no longer to get, but to give.

Working with the Text

A Life of Forgiveness (Colossians 3:12–13)

1. In **verse 12** Paul again reminds the Colossians that they are "God's chosen people, holy and dearly loved." Such reminders are scattered throughout the letter. What is the purpose of these reminders? What effect should they have on the Colossians' attitude toward and reception of Paul's advice?

2. In **verse 5** of this chapter, Paul lists five evils which must be put to death with the "earthly nature." In **verse 8** he lists five more. Now Paul lists five virtues which are to mark the Christian's life. List those five virtues and define each in your own words.

a.

b.

c.

d.

e.

3. In the same breath, Paul also urges the Colossian Christians to practice forgiveness. How is forgiveness actually an integral part of—or basis for—the five virtues Paul mentions?

A Life of Love and Peace (Colossians 3:14–15)

1. The word used here for love is "agape." This is the special love of concern and compassion which seeks the good of its object. *Agape* is undeserved love. This is the word used in **John 3:16**—one of the most beautiful descriptions of God's love for us. How does *agape* differ from the understanding of love most people have today? How is it possible for Christians to practice *agape*?

2. Paul encourages these Christians to "let the peace of Christ rule in your hearts." What is "the peace of Christ"? How can Christians be "at peace" amid dangers, hostility, tragedies, wars? What effect does such peace have on our feelings about ourselves and our relationships with others?

A Life of Worship and Thanksgiving
(Colossians 3:16–17)

1. According to **verse 16**, what does Christian worship involve? How does this compare with your own understanding of worship?

2. Here again is a reminder to be thankful. Explain how thanksgiving is an essential part of worship. What does the "name of the Lord Jesus" have to do with thanksgiving?

Applying the Message

On the Larger Scene

1. Look again at the list of Christian virtues you defined earlier, in question 2 under "A Life of Forgiveness." How do those virtues compare with the five you listed in the opening activity for this session?

Describe one way in which a Christian today might demonstrate each of these virtues.

a. Compassion

b. Kindness

c. Humility

d. Gentleness

e. Patience

2. Would it be a good idea for Christians to have some minimum standard of behavior, such as the list of virtues just mentioned, by which to measure and judge a person's faith? Why or why not?

3. Think about Christians that you know—either from world or national news accounts, or from personal experience—whom you think truly demonstrate "what it means to be a Christian." List some of the names that come to mind, and explain why these people stand out in your mind.

On a More Personal Level

Think about Paul's encouragement to practice Christian love (*agape*) and forgiveness. These virtues are often very difficult to practice.

1. Many Christians struggle with their inability to forgive someone who has deeply hurt them. The temptation for revenge is strong, our own power to set aside the hurt is not great, and guilt over the unforgiving attitude complicates the matter. What meaningful words could you offer to such people?

2. Likewise, all Christians struggle with the injunction to "love one another as Christ loved us." Sometimes, this simply seems impossible. There are some people whom we just don't like. Think of specific instances when you have been caught up in this dilemma. What would you *say* or *do* (if you are one of those struggling Christians) in such a situation?

Taking the Lesson Home

Review

Make today's portion of Colossians the basis for a daily meditation during the coming week. Receive God's forgiveness for specific times each day when you failed to show compassion, kindness, humility, gentleness, patience, forgiveness, love. Concentrate on Paul's words of assurance that you are "God's chosen people, holy and dearly loved." Let the confidence inspired by that promise strengthen and renew you for new efforts to practice Christ's love in your life and relationships.

Looking Ahead

Read all of **Colossians 3:1–4:1**. These verses are an extension of Paul's encouragement to live in love and service to others—specifically to members of our own family and household.

Working Ahead

Choose one or more of the following suggestions for additional study.

1. Read Paul's beautiful description of Christian love in **1 Corinthians 13**.

2. Make a list of Christian virtues evident in your home or congregation. How does your list compare with Paul's? What might you do to help build up the expression of Christian faith?

3. Study the news presented on television and in newspapers for reports of Christians who demonstrate their faith with lives of love and compassion. Try to assess the media's bias toward Christians and Christian faith. On the whole, are Christians viewed in a positive light, or do they come off as less than loving and compassionate?

4. Continue adding insights and reactions to your notebook about the apostle Paul.

Lesson 9

Christians at Home and at Work
(Colossians 3:18–4:1)

Approaching This Study

This section of Paul's letter is often referred to as rules for the Christian family. The early Christians expected Christ's return to be very soon. In light of this firm expectation, the most important concern for Christians was faithfulness and watchfulness. However, as the return of Christ was delayed, it became necessary to provide future Christians with models of Christian instruction and conduct. In this section of Colossians, Paul provides such a model for the Christian household.

The subject of families and the family has been recently a hot topic in the news. Much of this news is far from heartening. Hardly a day passes without a story of family violence, parental neglect, or child abuse blazing across newspaper and tabloid headlines. Countless books—many of them best-sellers—explore the various roots and manifestations of dysfunctional families, and offer survival tips for those unfortunate enough to be part of such families. Recent presidential campaigns have devoted hours of rhetoric to promises and plans for restoring "solid, wholesome family values" to the nation.

All of this makes abundantly clear two important truths—the family has a vital role in society and today's family desperately needs help.

Explore your own experiences with and feelings about family. First, reflect on your childhood for a few minutes. What is your favorite family memory of childhood? Briefly describe this below.

Now work with several other members of the group to discuss and then complete one of the following statements about families.

1. A family is . . .

2. An ideal family . . .

3. The biggest problem facing families today is . . .

4. The best advice for having a successful family is . . .

An Overview

Unit Reading

Read **Colossians 3:12–4:1**. This combines the previous session's material (**verses 12–17**) with today's section of the letter (**3:18–4:1**). Notice how essential the earlier verses are to a clear understanding of what Paul writes about Christian families and households.

The Message in Brief

Having carefully established a solid frame of reference-these were God's chosen people, clothed in Christ's love and forgiveness-and having urged the Christians to "do . . . all in the name of the Lord Jesus," Paul lays out rules for Christian families and households. In the name of Christ, wives will submit to husbands; husbands will love and respect wives; children will obey parents; parents will train and encourage children; slaves will obey masters; masters will show fairness to slaves.

Working with the Text

Wives and Husbands (Colossians 3:18–19)

Contemporary philosophers, both Greek and Roman, as well as Jewish teachers, wrote extensively concerning marriage and the family. The Stoic philosopher Epictetus, for example, spoke of knowing and doing what is right as a husband, father, wife, neighbor, ruler, and subject. Christians did not seek to change the social structure of their world. They sought rather to inject a new and higher relationship in the social order—namely, "as is fitting in the Lord."

1. In **verse 18** Paul urges wives to "submit to your husbands, as is fitting in the Lord." How would you interpret this injunction? What is significant about the phrase "in the Lord" and the fact that all these rules are being addressed to "God's chosen people, holy and dearly loved"? Do Paul's words apply to wives today?

2. Read **verse 19** and then study Paul's words to husbands in **Ephesians 5:25–33**. How are husbands to show love for their wives? Describe the kind of love Paul is talking about. Explain how this kind of love will interact with—and affect—the wives' submission to their husbands.

Children and Parents (Colossians 3:20–21)

1. The word used for children refers to children who are growing up, and therefore still in the care of their parents. In Paul's day, parents were considered part of the superior class of society, along with rulers and

masters. Children were part of the inferior class that included subjects and slaves. Note that Paul does not use the prevailing social custom as a reason for obedience. Why are Christian children to obey their parents? How does a clear understanding of a Christian family affect this command to children?

2. Look at Paul's advice to fathers in **verse 21**. Compare this with his words to the Ephesian Christians (**Ephesians 6:4**). How would you reword this verse to make it positive? Are we justified in substituting "parents" for "fathers"? Explain.

Slaves and Masters (Colossians 3:22–4:1)

The first two rules for the Christian household, relating to husbands and wives, parents and children, are very concise. The relationship between Christian masters and slaves calls for more detailed discussion from Paul. A greater dilemma had to be resolved here: namely, the freedom that a Christian slave had in Christ and his continuing social status as a slave. The question was even more acute when the slave holder had become a Christian. A more detailed discussion of slavery in New Testament times is provided in lesson 13.

1. What duties of slaves are indicated in **verses 22–25**? What virtues seem most important for slaves? How does all this relate to **Colossians 3:17**?

2. What quality of a master is most important according to **4:1**? How does the second part of this verse provide a reminder and guideline for masters? What do Paul's words about slaves and masters say to Christians in their work or professional life?

Applying the Message

On the Larger Scene

1. Think about Paul's words to wives, husbands, children, and parents in the light of family life today. How has family life changed since Paul's times? List some situations and factors in today's world that make successful family living difficult.

2. Considering those factors-and your discussion of wives, husbands, parents, and children—how would you define a "successful" or "ideal" family in today's world? Is this definition different from the one discussed earlier?

3. What is the most helpful advice you could give families today?
Husbands and wives:

Parents:

Children:

On a More Personal Level

1. List the best and the worst thing about your own experience growing up in a family. These won't be shared, but again, they may provide you with helpful insights.

2. On the basis of those personal experiences, and applying what you have learned from a study of Colossians 3—the entire chapter—what tips can help ensure success for your own family future?

3. Again, drawing on your personal experience and this Bible study, what would you say is the most important thing for Christian family members to practice?

Taking the Lesson Home

Review

Read again **verses 12–14** of **Colossians 3**. Think about how these verses apply to Christian families—wives, husbands, children, parents; and to employers and employees. Pray for an extra measure of God's forgiveness and strength so that you can relate Paul's words to your life at home and at work.

Looking Ahead

Read **Colossians 4:2–6**, Paul's final words of instruction to the Colossian Christians. Notice how Paul links this encouragement for prayer, thanksgiving, petition, and Christian witness, to **3:17**—which ends with "Giving thanks to God the Father" through the Lord Jesus.

Working Ahead

Choose one or more of the following suggestions for additional study.

1. Look up entries for "family," "parents," "children," in a Bible encyclopedia or dictionary to learn more about the structure of families and about the roles and responsibilities of family members in Old and New Testament times.

2. The apostle Paul never married or had children. How effective was he at advising husbands, wives, and children regarding Christian family life? Continue adding insights and thoughts about Paul to your notebook.

3. Visit local bookstores—Christian and secular—and browse through the volumes of material on families and parenting. Compare what you find in these books with Paul's words to Christian families.

Lesson 10

Always Praying and Witnessing (Colossians 4:2–6)

Approaching This Study

Paul is wrapping up his letter to the Colossians. He has one more thing to say to the church—one last bit of instruction—before he ends with personal news and notes. This final "teaching" section is about prayer and Christian witness.

Prayer is something that Christians often take for granted. It's almost a "given"—we hear the word "prayer" so often in church; we join other members in reciting prayers; we are asked to pray for others; we pray for ourselves. But why? What is prayer? Why is it essential to our relationship with God?

1. How would you define prayer?

2. Why is prayer essential to Christian faith?

3. Now take a quick survey of your own prayer life. Read each statement about prayer and then check the column that best describes your feelings and beliefs.

	Agree Strongly	Think So	Really Not Sure
1. Prayer changes things.			
2. My prayers change things.			
3. God hears and answers prayers.			
4. God hears and answers my prayers.			
5. Made-up prayers are more meaningful than ones read from a book.			
6. I put as much into my prayers for others as into those for myself.			
7. Prayer involves watching and listening as much as speaking.			
8. Prayer should involve specific words and thoughts.			
9. Thanks should always be part of prayer—even in crises or tragedies.			
10. Praying with others is as important as praying for others.			
11. It is important to believe strongly when you pray.			
12. I love to pray.			

An Overview

Unit Reading

Read **Colossians 4:2–6**. Pause briefly after each verse to consider the thought and/or request expressed by Paul. Notice how this section focuses on prayer and actions.

The Message in Brief

After providing various models of instruction and conduct for Christian households, Paul adds a number of additional admonitions addressed to the entire Christian community. He links these final admonitions to **3:17**, which ends with the words "Giving thanks to God the Father" through the Lord Jesus. In this section of the letter, Paul provides encouragement for prayer, thanksgiving, petition, and Christian witness.

Working with the Text

Prayer That Is Constant, Watchful, and Thankful (Colossians 4:2)

1. Two translations of the opening words of this verse are "Devote yourselves to prayer" and "Continue steadfastly in prayer." What was Paul saying in these words? Do you think he meant for the Colossians to take him literally?

2. A parable that Jesus told deals with perseverance in prayer (**Luke 18:1–8**). Read the parable now. What important point regarding prayer does Jesus make?

3. *The Living Bible* paraphrases "being watchful" to read "watch for God's answers." Why is this such an important element in prayer? What does it indicate about the person who is praying?

4. How can the Colossians, and all Christians, be "thankful" whenever they pray—no matter what they are praying for? How does a spirit of thankfulness help make our prayers more effective?

Prayer for the Gospel (Colossians 4:3–4)

Notice that Paul devotes two verses specifically to a request for prayers on his behalf. What is he asking for? Recall that, as he wrote this letter, Paul was imprisoned for preaching the Gospel. For what might we expect him to ask? How does praying for other people's success in spreading the Gospel help to strengthen our own efforts to do so?

Witnessing to the Gospel (Colossians 4:5–6)

1. Paul began his letter with a specific prayer for the Colossian Christians. Look again at **1:9–10**. What does he want for them? Using **1:28** and **2:3**, explain what he means by wise dealings with outsiders.

2. The phrase "let your conversation be always full of grace, seasoned with salt" is paraphrased in *The Living Bible* as "Let your conversation be gracious as well as sensible." What does this advice suggest about how we should speak and act toward non-Christians? What motive lies behind such behavior—apart from the very real motive that these are people who are loved by God and, as such, worthy of our love?

Applying the Message

On the Larger Scene

1. Do you think prayer has fallen into disuse or only half-hearted use by many Christians today? Try to defend your answer. What might help stir up enthusiasm about praying?

2. Think again about Paul's encouragement to "be wise in the way you act toward outsiders." How would you assess the way Christians are perceived by the media: newspapers, television reporters, magazines, etc.? What is behind their attitude?

On a More Personal Level

1. Take a second, careful look at the prayer survey you completed earlier. How would you rank your overall attitude toward and practice of prayer? What are some specific ways that you might enable prayer to become more of a part of your life?

2. How about your "witness" to others? Does the idea of talking about your faith make you excited? A bit uncomfortable? Downright embarrassed? Be honest with yourself. What are two specific ways in which you could talk about and show your commitment to Jesus in relationships with others?

Taking the Lesson Home

Review

Here's one step toward building a stronger life of prayer—pray about it. Strange as it may seem, praying is the best way to help your prayers. Start by reading again **Colossians 4:2–4**. Try to picture the apostle Paul and his eager urgency as he asks for prayer. Imagine how much prayer must have meant to him, for him to urge others to pray for him. Think about the gems of advice in these verses: "Devote yourselves," be "watchful and thankful." Try to incorporate that advice in your own efforts. Then watch!

Looking Ahead

Read **Colossians 4:7–18**—the conclusion of Paul's letter. This section is a personal aside that provides fascinating information about Paul and other early church leaders.

Working Ahead

Choose one or more of the following suggestions for additional study.

1. Look over the notebook you've been keeping on Paul. Try to pull together some of the observations and insights into a more complete picture of Paul—the apostle, the man, and his teachings.

2. Look up "prayer" in a dictionary, a Bible encyclopedia, a Bible dictionary. How do the definitions and explanations compare with your own understanding of prayer?

3. Look up "witness" in a dictionary and several Bible reference books. Try to write your own definition of the word, one that clearly explains just what it means to confess your faith in Christ.

Lesson 11

Greetings from the Team (Colossians 4:7–18)

Approaching This Study

The last section of Paul's letter is devoted to personal notes, greetings, and a final encouragement. Careful, thoughtful reading of Paul's conclusion, and a bit of background information regarding names and places, reveal fascinating insights into the early Christian church—the people who played key roles, and the conditions under which the church began to grow.

Imagine that you are among those early Christians to whom the letter was addressed. Paul's closing words have special meaning for you because you know the people and places he refers to. Your task is to personalize and convey the meaning of Paul's words to a church today—your church.

Study **Colossians 4:7–18** carefully. Read the information below about some people and places mentioned in these verses. Then rewrite and prepare to present a portion of Paul's closing words to your classmates. Three possible divisions of the conclusion (for group work) are **verses 7–9; 10–14; 15–18**.

The People

Tychicus: (TICK-uh-kus) Paul's friend and associate, probably from Ephesus. It's almost certain he traveled to Jerusalem with Paul because he had been chosen by the Asia Minor churches to take the money they had collected for needy Christians in Jerusalem. Tychicus was with Paul in Rome. Paul sent him to Colosse and later to Ephesus with letters he had written.

Onesimus: (Oh-NESS-uh-mus) A slave who belonged to Philemon, Paul's Christian friend in Colosse. Paul probably met Onesimus in Rome after he had run away from his master. During his time with Paul, Onesimus became a Christian. He traveled back with Tychicus, who carried Paul's letter to the Colossians.

Aristarchus: (air-i-STAR-kus) A Jewish Christian from Macedonia who was a friend and co-worker of Paul. He was with Paul on the missionary journey to Ephesus when the silversmiths started a riot. Aristarchus accompanied Paul to Jerusalem and later left with him for Rome. He stayed with Paul during his imprisonment in Rome.

Mark, cousin of Barnabas: The writer of the second Gospel. John Mark lived in Jerusalem, where his mother, Mary, allowed the Christians to meet in her house. Mark later went with his cousin Barnabas and Paul to Cyprus on Paul's first missionary journey. Because he left them halfway through the trip, Paul refused to take him along when they set out again. Instead, Mark went back to Cyprus with Barnabas. Later, Paul and Mark were reunited in Rome, and Paul described him as a loyal friend and helper.

Jesus Justus: A Jewish Christian who was one of Paul's co-workers. His Jewish name was Jesus; his Roman name, Justus.

Epaphras: (ee-PAF-rus) A Christian who founded the church at Colosse. Epaphras visited Paul when he was in prison in Rome and gave him news about the Colossian Christians. As a result of this news, Paul wrote his letter to the Colossians.

Luke: A Greek-speaking doctor who wrote the Gospel of Luke and the Acts of the Apostles. Luke was Paul's friend and traveled with him on some of his journeys. He was able to describe first-hand some things that Paul said and did. On these journeys, Luke was also able to learn from the apostles and early Christians much about Jesus' life and the beginnings of the church. Luke sailed to Rome with Paul and stayed with him while he was imprisoned there.

Demas: (DEE-mus) A Christian who was with Paul during his imprisonment in Rome. He later deserted Paul and went off to Thessalonica.

Nympha: (NIM-fuh) A Christian woman in Laodicea who volunteered her home as a meeting place for the church there.

Archippus: (ARE-kip-us) A Christian living in or near Colosse; he may be Philemon's son (see **Philemon 2**). Paul urged Archippus to fulfill his ministry, and refers to him as a "fellow soldier."

The Places

Laodicea: (lah-oh-duh-SEE-uh) A city in the Lycus Valley of present-day Turkey—the Roman province of Asia in New Testament times. Laodicea was situated at the intersection of two important roads. It grew prosperous from trade and banking. Paul's letter to the Colossians was intended for Laodicea as well. The Christian church there may have been started during the time Paul stayed at nearby Ephesus.

Hierapolis: (here-AP-poh-lus) A city in the Roman province of Asia, now western Turkey. Paul mentions the Christians here in his letter to nearby Colosse. Over the centuries, the hot-water springs at Hierapolis (modern Pamukkale) have "petrified to form amazing waterfalls of stone.

© (Information adapted from The Lion Encyclopedia of the Bible. Oxford: Lion Hudson plc, 1978.Pat Alexander, editor)

Use the space below to compose your section of Paul's personal news and final greetings.

An Overview

Unit Reading

After rewriting your section of Paul's closing words, read the entire conclusion: **Colossians 4:7–18**. As you read, apply what you've learned from the information provided in the previous section.

The Message in Brief

The concluding lines of Paul's letter to the Colossian Christians are filled with personal notes and greetings. This follows the pattern of all the Pauline letters. Even though he is in prison, the apostle makes no mention of his condition; Tychicus and Onesimus will inform the church as to how things are going with Paul. He asks the readers to remember his imprisonment. This final greeting is written in Paul's own hand.

Working with the Text

The Letter Carriers (Colossians 4:7–9)

1. How does Paul describe Tychicus? Read **2 Timothy 4:12** and **Titus 3:12**. In what capacity had Tychicus functioned? How is Tychicus described in **Ephesians 6:21**?

2. What does Paul say about Onesimus? The Onesimus mentioned by Paul in **Philemon 1–12** was a slave. (He will be studied in Lessons 12 and 13 of this course.) Most scholars believe that Onesimus the slave is the same Onesimus mentioned in **Colossians 4:9**. How does Paul describe him?

Greetings from Christians (Colossians 4:10–14)

1. Aristarchus is also mentioned in **Acts 19:29; 20:4;** and **27:2**. What do these passages tell you about the man? How might they also suggest why he was a prisoner with Paul?

2. After reading about the earlier rift between Paul and John Mark, how would you explain Paul's description of him in these verses? What does this indicate about Paul? About John Mark?

3. How do we know from these verses that Aristarchus, Mark, and Jesus were Jews? How did they serve Paul?

4. Epaphras had been associated with the Colossian Christians from the very beginning (**Colossians 1:7–8**). How does Paul describe Epaphras and his ministry?

5. Luke is with Paul as the apostle faces death (**2 Timothy 4:6–11**). Why would Luke be a good companion for Paul at such a time? What do these verses in the second letter to Timothy reveal about Demas?

Greetings to the Christian Community
(Colossians 4:15–18)

1. What were the Colossians to do with this letter from Paul? What were they to receive from the Laodicean congregation? There is to this day no trace of the Epistle to the Laodiceans, although Bible scholars have promoted various theories about its identity. Some scholars believe that Paul is referring to the letter to the Ephesians. Letters from an apostle were highly valued by the congregations. Copies would be made and circulated.

2. Why does Paul single out the woman Nympha for special greetings? In Paul's day there were no church buildings. Nympha is only one of the many early Christians who opened their homes as meeting places for local Christians. Others included Aquila and Priscilla in Ephesus (**1 Corinthians 16:19**) and later in Rome (**Romans 16:5**), Philemon in Colosse, and Gaius in Corinth (**Romans 16:23**).

3. Though most letters were written by scribes, it was customary in Paul's time to write the final words of a letter in one's own hand. Read the final verse of Colossians. How would these words—and the knowledge that Paul wrote them himself—impact his audiences? On the Colossians' attitude toward Paul?

Review of Colossians

Review several headings under "Working with the Text" in Lesson 1of this Study Guide. Look at the information under "What Prompted the Letter?" and "A Quick Overview of the Letter." Then briefly summarize the five divisions of Colossians in the following space.

Applying the Message

On the Larger Scene

1. Skim through the letter to the Colossians, noting the five divisions you listed above. Recall class discussions during the previous 10 lessons. Which part of this letter do you feel is most relevant to Christians in today's world? Explain your choice.

2. What tips about more effective communication could today's Christian churches learn from Paul's letter?

On a More Personal Level

1. Which sections of Paul's letter were most meaningful to you personally? Explain what you learned and how you might apply those lessons to your life.

2. Based on what you've studied in these lessons, compare the Christian church of Paul's time with the church today. Were there more problems and challenges then or now? How are the problems and challenges similar? Were

Christians more committed and enthused in Paul's day? Would you have liked to have been part of an early church group such as the Colossian Christians?

Taking the Lesson Home

Review

Read the entire letter to the Colossians in one sitting. As you read, reflect on the studies and discussions during the past weeks. Copy favorite sections of the letter into a notebook or on note cards and use these as the basis for daily meditations and prayers of thanks.

Looking Ahead

Read the letter to **Philemon**—the subject of the final two sessions in this course. This is a very brief letter (it's only 25 verses long), and it has a warm, intimate tone. As you read, keep in mind what you already know about Paul, about Onesimus (who likely accompanied the letter), and about the church in Colosse, to which Philemon belonged.

Working Ahead

Choose one or more of the following suggestions for additional study.

1. See what else you can discover in a Bible dictionary or encyclopedia about some of the people and places mentioned in Colossians: Colosse, Laodicea, Hierapolis, Tychicus, John Mark, Onesimus, Luke.

2. Continue to add interesting information to your notebook.

Lesson 12

Philemon—Background
(Philemon 1–7)

Approaching This Study

The letter to Philemon is private, personal correspondence from Paul to one of his good friends and converts. Philemon was likely a wealthy and important man in the town of Colosse, a man who owned a number of slaves. He had become a Christian through Paul's ministry; and he offered his home as a meeting place for the Colossian church. Philemon had gained a considerable reputation for his works of love toward fellow believers.

One of Philemon's slaves—Onesimus—had stolen some money and run away to Rome where he hoped to avoid being found. We're not told why Onesimus fled; but this was a serious offense in the Roman world. A slave was at the mercy of his master. The slightest offense was often severely punished. A runaway slave who was captured might be tortured and put to death as a lesson to other slaves.

Somehow, Onesimus came into contact with Paul while the apostle was imprisoned in Rome and, through this contact, Onesimus became a Christian. Though Paul was greatly helped by Onesimus' service and loved him like a son, the apostle realized that this slave must be returned to his owner. It must have been difficult for Paul—certainly it was difficult for Onesimus, who faced possible punishment—but the slave must return to face Philemon and make amends.

So Paul sent Onesimus back to Colosse—along with this "cover letter" and accompanied by Tychicus, who could provide company and moral support. The men also carried with them Paul's letter to the Colossian church.

That is the background to this unique letter from Paul. In preparation for a study of the epistle itself, try to imagine yourself in the situation.

1. Describe Philemon's dilemma and his probable feelings toward Onesimus, before he received Paul's letter. He was apparently a devout Christian; but he was still new to the faith and may not yet have fully grasped what Christian love entailed. Slaves were simply not thought of as people with rights and privileges. And, not only had Onesimus run away, he had also stolen money.

2. We are never told why Onesimus ran away or what kind of master Philemon was. Do these factors matter as far as Onesimus' actions are concerned?

3. Why do you think this personal letter is in our Bibles?

An Overview

Unit Reading

Read **Philemon 1–7**, the introduction to Paul's letter. Compare these opening words to Paul's greeting and introduction in the letter to the Colossian Christians.

The Message in Brief

Paul's opening words are warm and loving. He again identifies himself and Timothy as the writers of the letter, and greets Philemon, possible members of Philemon's family, and the church that meets in Philemon's home. Paul then offers words of praise and encouragement for the active faith shown by Philemon.

Working with the Text

Salutation and Greeting (Philemon 1–3)

1. Look at Paul's description of himself in **verse 1**. How is this different from his salutation in the letter to the Colossians? Considering Paul's purpose in this letter, what might account for the difference?

2. How does Paul characterize Philemon?

3. It is likely that Apphia was Philemon's wife and Archippus was their son. Note Paul's description of Archippus, and review his earlier mention in **Colossians 4:17**. On the basis of these two references, what do you learn about Archippus?

4. Since Paul was also (probably at the same time) sending a letter to the Colossian church, it may seem odd that he asks Philemon to greet them. In what way is the entire congregation involved in the matter of Philemon and Onesimus? What effect might this "reminder" have on Philemon's reception of what was to come?

Thanks and a Prayer (Philemon 4–7)

1. As with most of Paul's letters, the salutation is followed immediately by thanksgiving. Note the striking similarity between this thanksgiving and the one recorded in **Colossians 1:3–12** and **Philippians 1:3–11**. For what does Paul thank God when he prays about Philemon?

2. How has Philemon's love affected the congregation ("the saints")? What does Paul ask for Philemon?

3. How do you think this warm greeting and the words of praise and encouragement will affect Philemon's reception of what Paul will next ask him? Why are Paul's opening words not simply "good psychology" meant to manipulate Philemon into granting Paul's request? What can we learn from this about our own approaches to, and dealings with, other Christians?

Applying the Message

On the Larger Scene

1. Think about the way Paul tells Philemon he is praying for him. Compare this with our own prayers for other Christians, and with the way we do or don't tell them we are praying for them. What does it mean today when someone says, "I'll remember you in my prayers"? What sort of occasion usually prompts this promise? How is this different from Paul's practice of praying for others?

2. Paul is sending this letter to Philemon by the hands of Tychicus *and* *Onesimus*. He doesn't send the letter first and then, after getting Philemon's response, decide what to do with the runaway slave. What does this indicate about Paul's attitude toward Philemon? About his faith in Christ? How do Christians today take such risks on the strength of their faith?

3. Using Paul's actions regarding Onesimus as a model, briefly explain how Christians today can involve themselves in disputes between other Christians.

On a More Personal Level

1. Think about your own prayers for other Christians. What motive(s) usually prompt these prayers?

2. How often do you praise and encourage other Christians in their efforts for Christ? Why is a letter or written note of encouragement often more meaningful than a phone call or spoken message? To whom could you write such a letter? What would you include in the letter?

Taking the Lesson Home

Review

Study Paul's words to Philemon as a model for your prayers about others.

Looking Ahead

Read the entire letter to **Philemon**. Watch how Paul leads from his warm greeting into a loving, tactful request. Note the way he gently but firmly builds his case for Onesimus on the basis of Christian faith and love.

Working Ahead

Choose one or more of the following suggestions for additional study.

1. For further background to Paul's letter to Philemon, look up entries for "Philemon" and "Onesimus" in a Bible dictionary or encyclopedia; or read a commentary on the letter to Philemon.

2. Check a reference book (Bible handbook, Bible encyclopedia) to research the practice of slavery in New Testament times.

3. Begin to complete your notebook on the apostle Paul. The letter to Philemon provides additional information about Paul's character, his understanding of psychology and people, and his love for Jesus.

Lesson 13

Philemon—The Request
(Philemon 8–25)

Approaching This Study

Slavery was an accepted institution of the ancient world. The practice of buying, maintaining, and selling slaves was so widespread in the Roman Empire that possibly half the population lived as slaves. Since slaves often rebelled against their masters, stringent and cruel laws were passed to regulate slavery. Slaves had no rights under law. If a slave ran away (as Onesimus had done), a warrant was issued against him; and when apprehended, he was subjected to whatever punishment his master chose. Roman law decreed that if a master had been killed by a slave, the remaining slaves in that household—although innocent of a crime—could be put to death.

One of the few hopes for mercy a runaway slave might have was to find a friend of his master who would intercede for him. Onesimus found such a friend in Paul, his spiritual father in Christ—who also happened to be the spiritual father of his owner, Philemon.

Paul's purpose in writing was to beg Philemon to be lenient with Onesimus. It isn't clear whether Paul has thoughts about freeing Onesimus. He certainly does not specify this in the letter. What he does call for is a Christian sense of love and responsibility toward slaves, particularly when both master and slave are brothers in Christ.

1. How would you explain Paul's refusal to ask that Onesimus be set free?

2. Look at several other letters in which Paul mentions slaves: **1 Corinthians 12:13** and **Galatians 3:28**. Why would these statements have been considered "revolutionary" in Paul's day?

As you study Paul's request regarding Onesimus, notice how the thoughts in the previous verses form the basis for Paul's case to Philemon.

An Overview

Unit Reading

Read **Philemon 8–25**. Notice how Paul comes right to the point of his letter. Also, observe how carefully Paul puts his request. How would you describe the tone of Paul's words to Philemon?

The Message in Brief

Paul requests that Philemon be lenient with Onesimus—a very different man is returning to his master—a new person in Christ. Paul begs Philemon to welcome him back as such. The apostle points out that he could insist—he had the authority to do so, and Philemon was in his debt. But he trusts Philemon's faith and Christian love; he knows that Philemon will do all he asks—and more.

Working with the Text

The Request (Philemon 8–14)

1. Paul launches into his request with a reminder: "although in Christ I could be bold and order you to do what you ought." What does Paul mean by these words? Why does he choose not to do so?

2. What happened to Onesimus while Paul "was in chains"?

3. In **verse 11** Paul plays on Onesimus' name, which means "useful." What is he saying here?

4. Paul is not above using some personal pressure, reminding Philemon of his own (Paul's) stake in the fate of Onesimus. List phrases in **verses 9–13** that contribute to this pressure. Why might Paul use these phrases?

Motivation for Philemon (Philemon 15–20)

1. What does Paul seem to be suggesting in **verse 15**? (Is Paul encouraging Philemon to see the hand of God in all this: "perhaps the reason he was separated from you . . ."?) How would the relationship between Onesimus and Philemon be different now?

2. Notice again that Paul is writing part of the letter "with my own hand." This time, however, it is not simply the custom of the time that dictates such a personal touch. What is Paul's purpose in hand-writing this part of his letter to Philemon? What effect would this reassurance have?

3. Paul couples his promise to repay with yet another reminder: ". . . not to mention that you owe me your very self." Despite his words, Paul seems not the least bit hesitant to mention this debt. What do we owe one another in Christ?

4. In his conclusion to the appeal, Paul repeats a phrase he had used earlier in regard to Philemon's love for "the saints." How would Philemon's anticipated response "refresh" Paul's heart?

A Confident Greeting (Philemon 21–25)

Paul closes his letter with a beautiful note of confidence. Study his words in these verses. How does Paul demonstrate his confidence in Philemon?

his confidence in God?

his confidence in prayer?

Applying the Message

On the Larger Scene

Consider the Christian's responsibility regarding social and class issues today: racism, homelessness, prejudice against certain classes and minorities. How important are laws regarding these issues? What is the difference between such political approaches and the Gospel approach? What specific steps might a Christian take in effecting changes?

On a More Personal Level

1. Think about the sub-title of this course: "Take a New Look at Christ." Paul's letter to the Colossian Christians was written to help them with- stand certain heresies and threats to their faith. He wrote to Philemon in order to encourage loving and lenient treatment of a runaway slave. How does the title of the course summarize the emphasis of both these letters?

2. In what way does each of us need to take a new look—*a constantly new* look—at Christ?

3. On the basis of your work in this course, take a new look at Paul. What have you learned about this apostle? List his characteristics as a

Christian:

as a leader:

as a human being:

Taking the Lesson Home

Review

How could Paul's loving, Gospel approach to Philemon provide a model for your own efforts at bringing about reconciliation between Christians (especially if you are one of those Christians)? Pray for Christ's strength and love to motivate your life and your dealings with others.

Looking Ahead

Reread Paul's letters to the **Colossians** and **Philemon**. Use those letters and your notes from this course as the basis for family or personal meditations in the weeks ahead.

Working Ahead

Use the following suggestions for personal study.

1. Read the other New Testament letters of Paul: **Romans, 1** and **2 Corinthians, Galatians, Ephesians, Philippians, 1** and **2 Thessalonians, 1** and **2 Timothy, Titus**.

2. Check a Bible history book for further information about how the early Christian church grew and spread throughout the known world.

3. Find out more information on the apostle Paul—his early years as a Pharisee, his conversion, his missionary efforts, and his imprisonment.

COLOSSIANS
and
PHILEMON

Take a New Look at Christ

Leaders Notes

Leaders Notes

Preparing to Teach
Colossians and Philemon

Group Bible Study

Group Bible study means mutual learning from one another under the guidance of a leader or facilitator. The Bible is an inexhaustible resource. No one person can discover all it has to offer. In a class, many eyes see many things, and can apply them to many life situations. Leaders should resist the temptation to "give the answers" and thereby take on the role of an "authority." This approach stifles participation by individual members and can actually hamper learning. As a general rule, the leader is not to interpret, but to *develop interpreters*. Of course there are times when leaders should and must share insights and information gained by their own deeper research.

The ideal class is one in which the leader guides class members through the lesson, engages them in meaningful sharing and discussion at all points, and leads them to a summary of the lesson at the conclusion. As a general rule, try to avoid telling learners things that they can discover by themselves.

Have a chalkboard and chalk or newsprint and marker available to note significant points of the lesson. (The Leaders Guide often suggests ways in which these tools can be used.) Recast your observations about the lesson, or the observations of participants, into questions, problems, or issues. This stimulates thought and reflection. Keep discussion to the point. List on the chalkboard or newsprint the answers given. Then determine the most vital points made in the discussion. Ask additional questions to fill obvious gaps.

The aim of every Bible study is to help people grow spiritually, not merely in biblical and theological knowledge, but in Christian thinking and living. This means growth in Christian attitudes, insights, and skills for Christian living. The focus of this course must be the church and world of our day. The guiding question will be, "What does the Lord teach us for life today through these letters of Paul?"

Teaching the New Testament

Teaching a New Testament letter that was originally written for and read to first-century Christians can become merely ancient history if not applied to life in our times. Leaders need to understand the time and culture in which the letter was written. They need to understand the historical situation of the early church and the social and cultural setting in which that church existed. Such background information can clarify the original purpose and meaning of the letters and shed light on their meaning for Christians today. For this reason, it would be good to consult a number of commentaries and Bible reference works in preparation for class.

Teaching the Bible can easily degenerate into mere moralizing, in which do-goodism or rules become substitutes for the Gospel, and sanctification is confused with justification. Actually, justified sinners are moved, not by law, but by God's grace to a totally new life. Their faith is always at work for Christ in every context of life. Meaningful personal Christianity consists in a loving trust in God that is evidenced in love for others. Having experienced God's free grace and forgiveness, Christians daily work in their world to reflect the will of God for people in every area of human endeavor.

Christian leaders are Gospel-oriented, not Law-oriented; they distinguish between the two. Both Law and Gospel are necessary. The Gospel will mean nothing unless we first have been crushed by the Law and see our sinfulness. There is no genuine Christianity if faith is not followed by lives pleasing to God. In fact, genuine faith is inseparable from life. The Gospel alone gives us the new heart that causes us to love God and our neighbor.

Pace Your Teaching

Do not try to cover every question in each lesson. This would lead to undue haste and frustration. Be selective. Know your class members and pace your teaching accordingly. Allot approximately 10 minutes to the introduction and two or three minutes for the overview. Take time to explore the biblical text paragraph by paragraph, but not verse by verse or word by word. Get the sweep and continuity of meaning. Stop occasionally to help participants gain understanding of a word or concept. Allow 15–20 minutes to apply the lesson, and about five minutes for "Taking the Lesson Home." This suggested schedule, you will notice, leaves only 30 minutes for working with the text. If most members study the text at home (as suggested at the end of each lesson in the Study Guide), they can report their findings, and the time gained can be used to apply the lesson to life.

Should your group have more than a one-hour class period, you can ease the pace and proceed with more leisure. But do not allow any lesson to "drag" and become tiresome. Keep things moving. Keep the class alive. Keep the lesson meaningful.

Good Preparation

Using Resources

Good preparation by the leader usually affects the pleasure and satisfaction the class will experience. The student or teacher cannot get the background—historical, cultural, and theological—for such books as Paul's letters to the Colossians and Philemon by reading only the biblical text. Paragraphs, sentences, phrases, individual words and expressions can be understood fully only in light of the times and circumstances in which the apostle wrote. Thus it is important that both student and class leader consult introductory articles in reference works and commentaries. Also read the text in a modem translation. The NIV is generally referred to in the lesson comments. The NIV shows clear paragraph divisions, the structure of the letters, and the original form in which Paul wrote the epistles.

Congregations can provide leaders with some essential books by purchasing them for the church library or for the individual teacher's library. The following resources are especially recommended:

- a good, recently revised Bible dictionary or encyclopedia;
- a thorough Bible commentary, such as *The People's Bible* from Concordia Publishing House;
- one or more recent translations and paraphrases of Paul's letters: NIV, NRSV, Phillips, *The Living Bible*.

Personal Preparation

Good teaching directs the learners to discover for themselves. For the leader, this means directing learners, not giving answers. As you prepare, mark those sections which suggest an activity most suitable for your class. Choose verses that should be looked up in Scripture. Decide which discussion questions you will ask, and which you will devote most time to. Write these in the margins of your Leaders Guide. Highlight the Study Guide questions and application activities that you'll emphasize. What practical actions could you propose for the week following the lesson? Which suggestions in the Study Guide do you feel are most appropriate for your class? Mark these in your book.

Plan brief opening and closing devotions. Either use the suggestions provided in the Leaders Guide, or make up your own devotions. As much as possible—especially after the first sessions, when participants may still feel uncomfortable-involve class members in these devotions.

How will you best use your teaching period? Do you have 45 minutes? An hour? Or 1 ½ hours? If time is short, what should you cut? Learn to become a wise steward of class time.

Perhaps most important of all, be sure to begin your preparations for each session with personal prayer. Ask for God's wisdom, direction, and insight so that your mind is freed to focus on the biblical material and what it says to your life. When the text becomes clear to you, when Paul's words have meaning for *your* life, you will find it exciting—exhilarating—to help your class members discover how these letters speak to them.

Suggestions for Using the Study Guide
The Lesson Pattern

This set of 13 lessons is based on significant and timely New Testament writing—Paul's letters to the Colossian Christians and to Philemon. The Study Guide material is designed to aid Bible study: that is, to a consideration of the written Word of God, with discussion and personal application growing out of the text at hand.

The typical lesson is divided into five sections:

1. Approaching This Study
2. An Overview
3. Working with the Text
4. Applying the Message
5. Taking the Lesson Home

"Approaching This Study" is meant to arouse the group's interest in the content and concepts of the Bible section to be studied. Open-ended questions, surveys, or "ranking" exercises are often employed to attract participants' interest and whet their curiosity about the lesson material that will follow. Do not linger too long on these introductory activities, but do keep them in mind for later reference as you plunge into the actual biblical material. Their purpose—apart from stimulating interest—is to show that Paul's letters are meaningful to the lives of your class members.

"An Overview" offers a capsule understanding of the textual material covered in the session. Before the text is broken down for closer scrutiny, it should be seen in context—as part of the whole. At this point, the class leader takes the participants to "higher ground" and shows them the general layout of the biblical material. The overview gives the group an idea where it is going, what individual places are to be visited, and how the two are interrelated.

"Working with the Text" provides the real "spade-work necessary for the Bible study. Here the class digs, uncovers, and discovers; it gets the facts and takes a close look at them. Comments from the leader are necessary only to the extent that these help the group more clearly understand the text. The same is true of looking up any indicated parallel passages. The questions in the Study Guide, arranged under topical sub-headings related to the Bible content, are intended to help learners discover the text's original meaning and impact.

"Applying the Message." Having determined what the text says, the class is ready to discover its message for them, for their lives as Christians. This is done, as the Study Guide suggests, by taking the truths from Paul's letters and applying them to the world and Christianity in general, and then to the participants' personal lives. Class time will probably not permit thorough discussion of all questions and topics. In preparation, leaders may want to select two or three from each category—ones that seem most relevant to their class members—and focus on these. Be sure to include questions from the "On a More Personal Level" category, since they are meant to bring God's message to the individual Christian. Close this section by reviewing one important truth from the lesson.

"Taking the Lesson Home" supplies stimulated participants with guidelines for enrichment work at home. Suggestions are given for personalized review, for preview of the following lesson, and for private study of topics related to the lesson. Be sure to give class members who complete some of these activities the chance to report on their findings during the next session.

Remember, the Word of God is sacred, but the Study Guide is not. The guide offers only suggestions. Don't hesitate to alter the suggestions or to substitute other ideas that will better meet your own needs and the needs of the participants. Adapt your teaching plan to your own class and your class period.

Lesson 1

Greetings from Paul (Colossians 1:1–2)

Lesson Aim

This introductory lesson opens with a brief exploration of the New Testament letters. Why are they important? How and why were they written? What format, content, and method of communication did they typically employ? As you move through this overview, participants will examine their knowledge and understanding of these Bible books. The lesson then concentrates on the letter to the Colossian Christians. Participants will focus on Paul, the author of Colossians, (What do they really know about him? Why was he such a powerful leader in the early Church?) and begin to explore the thrust of the letter (What does it reveal about the early Christians in Colosse?) and its message for Christians today-specifically, its application to their own lives and relationships within the church.

Lesson Objectives

By the power of the Holy Spirit working through God's Word, the participants will

1. examine their knowledge and understanding of the New Testament letters;

2. share discoveries about the apostle Paul and his purpose in writing to the Colossian Christians;

3. describe and react to ways in which God communicates with them-through His Word;

4. begin to assess their own role in sharing God's Word with fellow Christians.

Opening Worship

If possible, bring to class a list of prayer requests from your church newsletter or bulletin. Talk with the group about the people mentioned in the list. Invite additional prayer requests from other participants. Then spend several minutes in a silent, group prayer for the people named.

Conclude by praying aloud:

Almighty and all-loving God and Father, open our eyes and our hearts to the message of Your Word. Give us ready minds and a spirit of eagerness to explore the ways You speak to us today. Give us

thankfulness for the wisdom and courage of leaders such as Paul, and an understanding that will translate his ancient words into timeless encouragement for our own lives. Most of all, give us Your own spirit of love so that all we do is prompted by an outpouring of the great love You showed us through Jesus. Amen.

Approaching This Study

For this and some future lessons, it might be helpful to have on hand recent newsletters and information pieces from your congregation, as well as letters or periodicals from the church-at-large. These pieces can prompt discussion and comparison as you discuss New Testament letters, Paul's letter to the Colossians, and written communication in the church today. If possible, display these so participants can browse before class and refer to them at specific points during the lesson.

Direct participants to the Study Guide. Read aloud the opening paragraph. Then let participants skim through the New Testament letters in their Bible and discuss what they know about them. Keep the discussion brief. The point of this activity is to assess the group's familiarity with these unique books.

The next paragraphs in the Study Guide describe an important emphasis of this course. All the New Testament epistles can be enriched by an awareness that they are letters, and by a careful examination of the personal elements inherent in any letter.

An Overview

Unit Reading

Ask for a volunteer to read Paul's greeting aloud while other participants follow along in their Bibles.

The Message in Brief

You may wish to summarize the verses by noting the key elements in Paul's greeting on the chalkboard or a sheet of newsprint: author—Paul (an apostle of Jesus) and Timothy; reader or recipient—the Christians at Colosse; good wishes or greeting.

Let participants discuss the purpose of these elements. Beyond the simple task of identifying himself and addressing the letter, Paul offers a reminder of his authority, as an apostle of Jesus, and he establishes a warm, loving tone with his words of blessing.

Working with the Text

Either work through these sections with the entire group or divide the class into three groups to study and discuss the three headings: Who Were the Colossians? Who Was Paul? and What Prompted the Letter? If working in groups, allow about 10 minutes for reading and discussion; then call everyone together to share discoveries.

Who Were the Colossians?

If possible, refer to a map of the New Testament world to point out the cities of Rome (the site of Paul's imprisonment and the probable place where Paul wrote the letter) and Colosse (note the nearby city of Ephesus). Additional material about Colosse may be helpful: It had once been called a great city, but by Paul's time, Colosse was considered merely a "town." Located in what is now Turkey, it was inhabited by Greeks and settled by several thousand Jews from Mesopotamia and Babylon in the second century. Colosse was famous for its woolen and weaving industry. During the reign of Nero (AD 44–69), the town was destroyed by an earthquake and never rebuilt.

1. Paul's comments in **3:5–4:1** indicate some of the social and cultural pressures felt by the Colossian Christians. They were surrounded by sexual immorality, greed, idolatry, slander and lies, filthy language, and poor models of family and household relationships. In these verses, Paul offers encouragement and specific advice for withstanding such pressures.

2. In **1:12–14** and **2:13–14**, Paul reminds the Colossians of their release from sin and darkness through Christ, the gift of forgiveness, and their place in Christ's kingdom. As participants express these blessings in their own words, let them also reflect on how such a reminder can help them withstand pressures in their own lives.

Who Was Paul?

1. Once participants have fleshed out the basics of Paul's story (his background; his conversion; his reputation as a great missionary, church leader, and letter-writer), concentrate on personal knowledge of and feelings about the apostle. Is Paul someone whom participants would like to know? One great way to get to know this man is by reading things he wrote—in addition to things written *about* him. Paul's letters—Colossians and Philemon among them—contain all sorts of interesting clues about the man and his faith.

The Christians in Colosse had never met Paul. His letter to them had a double task: he needed to establish a relationship of trust and love that would foster a spirit of openness to and acceptance of the advice he offered.

Encourage participants to watch how Paul builds that relationship in the words he chooses.

2. Paul's conversion experience left a powerful, permanent impression and conviction regarding his new role as an ambassador of Jesus.

As you discuss Paul's imprisonment, refer again to the map to indicate the cities of Rome (from which Paul most likely wrote the letters to Colossians, Philemon, and Ephesians) and the cities of Colosse and Ephesus, to which Tychicus and Onesimus carried the letters.

What Prompted the Letter?

1. Take time to discuss and understand the threats to the Christian community that were coming from the Judaizers and the Gnostics. On the one hand, the temptation was to earn God's good favor by keeping certain aspects of Old Testament ceremonial law. On the other, the Gnostics were trying to bring Christianity in line with popular Greek philosophy—a system of ideas that claimed spirit to be good and material things to be evil. You might compare these errors mentioned to similar beliefs and practices today.

2. Affirm salvation as a *gift*—something which was won for us by Jesus' death on the cross and is freely offered to them through faith. This is what grace is all about. Human nature does not respond well to grace, because it seems to go against everything that makes sense. Grace is at the very heart of the Christian faith—God, in Christ, loved us so much that He freely wipes away everything evil that we've done and offers us eternal membership in His family.

A Quick Overview of the Letter

Call attention to the chart in the Study Guide. This indicates a five-section division of the letter to Colossians. Suggest that participants use the chart to record notes and observations about the letter as they read and discuss it in future lessons.

Applying the Message

On the Larger Scene

1. Participants may have personal experiences in which they encountered teachings or attitudes that seemed to conflict with Christianity. It is certain that everyone has experienced the pull of legalism (*"I've got to do something to*: please God/make myself a better person/justify the way God answered my prayer/make up for the way I acted last week/etc."). There is nothing at all wrong with trying to improve our behavior and attitude; in fact, this is something that pleases God. But the motivation must not be an effort to win favor; rather, it should flow naturally in response to the Gospel.

2. How do participants feel about the need to speak out against error today? There is certainly such a need. Stress the importance of approaching those who are teaching incorrectly, and of prayerfully utilizing all the wisdom, discernment, and love that God can give us in such matters.

On a More Personal Level

1. Encourage frank and open discussion. Stress Paul's overriding purpose of building up the church in love.

2. Paul's words indicate a caring, loving relationship. Even though Paul had never met many of the Colossian Christians, he respected them and wanted to encourage them in their faith. Invite participants to assess their own church relationships honestly. God's grace and forgiveness is always available for those times when we fail or when our relationships are far from perfect.

Taking the Lesson Home

Encourage everyone to complete the Review activity, the Looking Ahead activity, and one or both of the Working Ahead activities prior to the next session.

Closing Worship

Conclude with a prayer of thanksgiving and encouragement. Begin by mentioning several specific spiritual blessings you have observed in your group today: eagerness to learn, willingness to tackle tough questions, love for one another or for the church as a larger body. Invite other participants to volunteer words of thanks for attitudes or efforts they have seen in the congregation or in the group. End the prayer yourself by thanking God for the free gift of Jesus and the eternal life He won for everyone.

Lesson 2

Thankfulness and Prayer (Colossians 1:3–14)

Lesson Aim

In this lesson you will examine Paul's use of prayer to express thanks and to ask for blessings; you also will hear Paul's reminder and encouragement to grow in your own prayer life as the Holy Spirit works through the Gospel, using every opportunity to explore and express a spirit of thankfulness.

Lesson Objectives

Through God's Word, the participants will

1. explore their experiences with and attitudes toward thankfulness;

2. identify and evaluate Paul's reasons for giving thanks in his prayer for the Colossians;

3. assess their own and the church's use of thanksgiving and affirmation today;

4. outline ways to develop a more thankful attitude in their own lives.

Opening Worship

If possible, bring to class a cassette recorder and a tape of songs of praise; "Now Thank We All Our God," "How Great Thou Art," etc. Explain that this lesson focuses on thanksgiving and prayers of thanks. Then play the tape, inviting participants to sing along if they wish.

Another alternative is simply to read or sing together the beautiful old hymn of praise "How Great Thou Art."

O Lord my God, when I in awesome wonder
Consider all the works Thy hand hath made,
I see the stars, I hear the mighty thunder,
Thy pow'r throughout the universe displayed;
Then sings my soul, my Savior God, to Thee,
How great Thou art! How great Thou art!
Then sings my soul, my Savior God, to Thee,
How great Thou art! How great Thou art!

But when I think that God, His Son not sparing,
Sent Him to die, I scarce can take it in,
That on the cross my burden gladly bearing
He bled and died to take away my sin,
Then sings my soul, my Savior God, to Thee,
How great Thou art! How great Thou art!
Then sings my soul, my Savior God, to Thee,
How great Thou art! How great Thou art!

Approaching This Study

Direct participants to the Study Guide and read aloud the first paragraph. Then allow time for class members individually to evaluate their attitudes and experiences with thankfulness by taking the survey.

Use the survey as a basis for a brief discussion of thankfulness. List the numbers 1–10 on the chalkboard or a sheet of newsprint. Then, when everyone has completed the survey, read each statement aloud and ask for a show of hands if participants have checked it in their books. Note the number of "checks" next to each number on the board. Let the class talk about their experiences with and observations of thankfulness in general. Could our society be described as thankful? How about the Christians whom they know? What are some obstacles that often thwart a spirit of thankfulness in today's world?

An Overview

Unit Reading

Read aloud or have a volunteer stand and read aloud **Col. 1:3–14**. Again, try to capture the sense of time and place and the anticipation that accompanied the original reading of this letter from Paul.

The Message in Brief

This section of the letter is a kind of bridge or lead-in to the weightier issues that Paul will address. After participants have had time to reflect on the questions and jot some notes, let them quickly summarize the contents of these verses: words of thankfulness, encouragement, and a reminder to the Colossian Christians. Note how carefully Paul weaves these elements into the framework of his prayers. This section is a positive affirmation that should make the Colossians themselves feel thankful (for Paul's praise and loving concern, for Paul's prayers about them, for the reminder of the gifts God had given them) and should prepare them to receive his later words with openness and willingness.

Working with the Text

You might want to divide the class into three groups and assign each group one of the sections described by the headings "The Prayer of Thanksgiving," "Paul Prays for the Colossians," and "Paul's Reminder about Thanksgiving." Allow time for the groups to read, discuss, and write brief answers to the questions in the Study Guide. Then discuss each section with the entire class, having the groups report their findings.

The Prayer of Thanksgiving (Colossians 1:3–8)

1. Paul is thankful for the Colossians' faith in Jesus and for the love they have shown for one another. These words provide wonderful reinforcement and encouragement. Paul emphasizes that the love springs from the

Christian's relationship with Jesus. Love and faith are both offshoots of the Gospel message or "word of truth" that was preached to the church in Colosse.

2. Paul's words about the "gospel that has come to you" directs the Colossians to the source of their faith and love, and reminds them of the power that has enabled them to grow in faith and love. His words are not empty flattery. Apart from the power that comes from Jesus, the Colossians would not be able to demonstrate such love and faith.

3. Paul considered Epaphras a "fellow servant" and "faithful minister of Christ on our behalf." Paul apparently had great respect and trust for this man. Epaphras also kept Paul apprised about the life and growth of the Colossian Christians. He had reported good things about the Colossians' great love for others—love which was inspired by the Holy Spirit.

Paul Prays for the Colossians (Colossians 1:9–11)

Paul asks that God will continue to bless the faith and love of these Christians. He asks God to give them knowledge of God's will—spiritual wisdom and understanding. Both the thanksgiving and the request are directed to the source of these people's spiritual growth—the Gospel. Let participants share thoughts on how the Colossians might be moved, encouraged, and strengthened by knowing that Paul is continually praying for them. Encourage volunteers to describe ways in which they have been encouraged and cheered by knowing that others were praying for them.

Paul's Reminder about Thanksgiving (Colossians 1:12–14)

1. These words urge the Colossians to continually thank God for the gift of faith, for life in God's family, and for the blessings of redemption and forgiveness of sins. Thanksgiving or a thankful spirit are—like grace—at the heart of Christian faith. In prayers of thanks, Christians have the opportunity to respond to God's love. In genuine thanksgiving, two vital things are present: we acknowledge God as the source of all good gifts, of our very lives; and we truly receive these as *gifts*—God's grace. When we lack thankful hearts, we fail to see the truth that faith is a gift from God. When this occurs, we are most tempted to try working out our own salvation, when we begin to judge ourselves and others on the basis of what we have or have not done, and when we are most vulnerable to false teaching.

2. Answers will vary for these questions, since participants are asked to use their own words. You might consider the difference between giving light and reflecting light. The sun and moon are often used as examples. Christians are to reflect the light of Christ in their daily lives. Light as opposed to darkness indicates a fundamental difference—we are to be as different from the people of the world as light is different from darkness. Redemption refers to an act which has already been accomplished. The

Greek word for redemption designates liberation from imprisonment. Stress the truth that for a Christian, redemption is forgiveness-purchased back from sin.

Applying the Message

On the Larger Scene

1. The light/darkness imagery is certainly appropriate to describe today's world. As was true with the Colossian Christians, faith demonstrates itself in selfless acts of love. Encourage participants to cite examples of "light" from news reports or from their own experiences. Deeds of love will call attention to individual Christians, but will also point beyond or through them to God as the power and source of light.

2. Let class members describe instances of affirmation, and lack of affirmation, that they have heard or experienced in their own lives. Is the act of affirmation unique to Christians? How might Christians help to build a spirit of affirmation? How will the power of forgiveness help Christians restore and rebuild in situations that are less than affirming?

On a More Personal Level

All the questions in this section require frank and honest sharing. It would be good to divide the class into small groups. Let each group work through the questions by talking and sharing thoughts. Allow enough time for all groups to discuss and make notes, then reassemble to discuss the results with the whole class. As you talk about the questions, move the discussion along positive, constructive lines. Participants can benefit from pooling thoughts and discoveries with the entire class.

1. Briefly review the results of the earlier survey. Share thoughts about how and why they have developed such feelings and attitudes. How might the church influence such feelings in a positive, affirming way?

2. Some typical barriers to thankfulness are worry, stress, insecurity, misfortune. How could the experience of forgiveness and the knowledge of God's grace help to break down some of these barriers?

3. A "thankful spirit" comes from genuine understanding of what God has done for us in Christ. If we can remove the barriers to such an understanding, our attitudes toward ourselves and our world will become more positive. Once we acknowledge that God is in control, and once we begin to focus on the gifts He has given, and continues to give us, we can reduce our anxiety about all the things we want to grasp for ourselves, through our own efforts.

4. Encourage groups to talk about how they have personalized and elaborated on each of the idea starters listed in the Study Guide. All of the suggestions can be helpful, but some might be more effective than others for

certain individuals. Remind participants that God provides means—His Word and Sacrament—to strengthen faith, enabling and empowering Christians to respond with thankful hearts.

Taking the Lesson Home

Encourage participants to complete the Review activity, the Looking Ahead activity, and one or more of the Working Ahead suggestions prior to the next lesson. If there is time now or in future lessons, let individuals share discoveries or observations they have noted about the apostle Paul in their notebooks.

Closing Worship

Ask participants to list some events or observations—either from this class session or from their personal lives-which might be mentioned in a prayer of thanksgiving. Note these on the chalkboard or a sheet of paper. Then conclude with a prayer devoted exclusively to giving thanks. If these were not mentioned in the list, be sure to offer thanks for the free gift of God's own Son: His life on earth, His suffering and death as punishment for our sins, and the forgiveness and eternal life that He won for us.

Lesson 3

A Picture of Christ (Colossians 1:15–23)

Lesson Aim

In this lesson you will examine and affirm Paul's clear proclamation of Jesus as God/man and Savior and explore what that proclamation means for Christians of all times.

Lesson Objectives

By the power of the Holy Spirit working through God's Word, the participants will

1. confirm their personal faith in Jesus;

2. examine and discuss Paul's beautiful description of Christ to the Christians at Colosse;

3. apply Paul's proclamation of Jesus as God/man and Savior to their lives.

Opening Worship

Invite participants to join you in confessing faith in Jesus, using the words of the Apostles' Creed:

I believe . . . in Jesus Christ, His only Son, our Lord, who was conceived by the Holy Spirit, born of the virgin Mary, suffered under Pontius Pilate, was crucified, died, and was buried. He descended into hell. The third day He rose again from the dead. He ascended into heaven and sits at the right hand of God the Father Almighty. From thence He will come to judge the living and the dead.

If anyone has brought to class a favorite hymn of thanksgiving (suggested in last lesson's "Working Ahead" ideas), invite them to use it as an opening prayer and, if they are willing, to explain why the hymn is particularly meaningful to them.

Approaching This Study

Direct participants to the opening paragraphs in the Study Guide. Read these aloud or let a volunteer read them. Refer to the opening worship in which participants confessed their beliefs in and about Jesus by using words of the Apostles' Creed.

Divide the class into groups of four or five and allow time for the groups to discuss and then write their descriptions. When everyone has finished, call on a member from each group to read the description members have developed. You might want to note recurring statements on the chalk-board or a sheet of newsprint for later comparison with Paul's words about Christ to the Colossians.

An Overview

Unit Reading

Ask a volunteer to read aloud **Colossians 1:15–23**, pausing briefly after each descriptive statement about Christ.

The Message in Brief

Read this paragraph aloud. Invite participants to recall what they discussed during lesson 1 about the background to the church at Colosse and Paul's reason for writing to the Christians there. You may want to have several individuals flesh out this material by rereading the material under "Who Were the Colossians?" and "What Prompted the Letter?" from "Working with the Text" in lesson 1.

Ask for responses to the question about comparing this section of the letter with what went before it. Do they find the tone more somber, even awesome? What words or phrases contribute to this tone?

Working with the Text

Complete this section with the entire class, pausing to let individuals jot brief answers to the questions before you discuss them with the class. Or divide the class into small groups to read and answer the questions before discussing the section with everyone.

The Christ Hymn (Colossians 1:15–20)

1. Let participants describe their reactions to these verses as a hymn. How would it fit into today's hymnbook? Under which section would they place it in their hymnbook? Hymns were important to early Christians not only as a vehicle for worship and praise, they were invaluable teaching devices—clarifying truths about the faith and unifying the doctrines of the church.

2. Both Adam and Christ have been described in the Bible as bearing the image of God. Christ is a "second Adam" in that He restored the purity of the image which Adam lost by sinning. The verses reveal that in Christ God shows us what He is like. In Christ—in His person, His life, His teachings, His work for us—we can see God's character and love for us. The reference to Christ's action in creation reveal that He is truly God.

3. Let participants speculate on the image of the church as a human body with Christ as its head. How appropriate is this image? As "head," Christ controls the functioning of all the body parts and unites them into one living, active, effective being. Because Christ is directing the body, all parts should work in harmony toward a common purpose.

4. In His resurrection, Christ proclaimed victory over death—the physical and eternal death that resulted from sin. The term "firstborn" implies a position of honor. Through faith, we are made part of God's family—siblings who are also "born from the dead." Invite participants to express the significance of this knowledge for them.

5. Through His death as payment for our sins, Christ removed the barrier that separated us from God and His love. Our sins are forgiven; we are made holy before God. We are now part of God's family—If class members are willing, let them discuss what this reconciliation means or has meant in their lives, in their feelings about themselves, in their attitudes toward others.

Reconciliation (Colossians 1:21–22)

1. The Colossian Christians had been separated from God by their sin. Through His death for those—and all—sins, Christ paid the punishment, wiped away their sins. Christ's reconciliation freed them from slavery to evil and turned them into people whose lives gave evidence that they now belonged to God. Because Christ had taken away their sins, the Colossians could now come before God free from sin. Imagine the difference this would

make in their attitude and approach to God. Let participants speculate on the effect this knowledge would have on the Colossians' feelings about and prayers to God, on their feelings about themselves and others.

2. Only animals that were perfect and without blemish were considered worthy offerings for God. God expects and deserves perfection. Through Christ we are perfect and without blemish. It is important, however, to remember that our new, blameless state is a *gift*—not something we've brought about. We remain holy only because Christ's sacrifice for us is for all time; when we acknowledge this and repent of our sins, God continues to see us as holy and blameless.

A Cautionary Note (Colossians 1:23a)

God assures us in His Word that salvation is ours through faith in Jesus. In these words, Paul cautions the Colossians—and us—not to run away, not to reject this wonderful gift by turning our backs on it. Do Christians sometimes turn their back on grace by taking it for granted and returning to their evil lives? What does such behavior say about their attitude toward God's grace and forgiveness?

A Personal Note from Paul (Colossians 1:23b)

Here again Paul reminds the Colossians that they had heard the Gospel message. These reminders reinforce and clarify what Paul had already taught. And he (once again) reminds them of his authority in the matter: he was a servant of the Gospel. Why does Paul insert his credentials?

Applying the Message

On the Larger Scene

Work together with the class to answer these questions. Encourage the sharing of thoughts and ideas as you talk through possible answers.

1. Sometimes, people can have a great deal of intellectual knowledge about Jesus or Christianity and fail to assimilate it personally, to let it affect their lives. As was mentioned earlier in the lesson, a personal relationship with Jesus is essential to Christian faith. However, it is also important to know just what and whom you are building this relationship on.

2. If we emphasize Christ's divine nature to the exclusion of His human nature, we fail to appreciate the enormity of God's love—which led Jesus to humble himself to become human, to experience joy, hardship, fear, anger, pain, death. Christ became human because humans are important to Him—all humans.

If we forget or fail to remember Christ's divinity, however, we can diminish the significance of his work and its effect for us. Only God could effect such miraculous results by suffering and dying; only God could overcome death and thereby guarantee eternal life for us.

On a More Personal Level

These questions ask for and require individual consideration. Allow everyone enough time to work independently through the questions. Then ask for volunteers to share their thoughts as you discuss these. There are no "correct" answers, but it will be helpful to listen and react to the responses of various individuals.

1. Encourage a number of participants to talk about their choice. This is a wonderful way to get to know more about the spiritual lives and feelings of one another.

2. Again, encourage open discussion. Let participants react to one another's answers and add their own thoughts.

3. Invite volunteers to share their responses.

Taking the Lesson Home

Encourage participants to complete the Review activity, the Looking Ahead activity, and one or more of the Working Ahead suggestions prior to next session. Again, if there is time, let individuals share discoveries or observations that have resulted from previous "homework."

Closing Worship

Read together **Col. 1:15–20** as a confession of faith.

If several participants brought along favorite hymns of praise and thanksgiving, invite them to read and discuss them at this time.

Lesson 4

*Job Description—Minister, Servant of the Gospel
(Colossians 1:24–2:5)*

Lesson Aim

God's call to preach and teach the Good News about Jesus is both rewarding and fraught with challenges. God calls every Christian to share the Gospel. With His call, God also sends the power and resources to carry out His mission effectively.

Lesson Objectives

By the power of the Holy Spirit working through God's Word, the participants will

1. list their attitudes about God's expectations for His children-to share the Gospel with all people.

2. read and then express in their own words Paul's description of his call and ministry;

3. describe some of the challenges and rewards that result from lives of Christian service;

4. commit themselves to strengthening their own efforts to tell others about Jesus.

Opening Worship

As an opening prayer, read stanzas 1, 2, and 5 of the hymn "Thy Strong Word."

Thy strong word did cleave the darkness;
At Thy speaking it was done.
For created light we thank Thee,
While Thine ordered seasons run.
Alleluia! Alleluia! Praise to Thee who light dost send!
Alleluia! Alleluia! Alleluia without end!

Lo, on those who dwelt in darkness,
Dark as night and deep as death,
Broke the light of Thy salvation,
Breathed Thine own life-giving breath.
Alleluia! Alleluia! Praise to Thee who light dost send!
Alleluia! Alleluia! Alleluia without end!

Give us lips to sing Thy glory,
Tongues Thy mercy to proclaim,
Throats that shout the hope that fills us,
Mouths to speak Thy holy name.
Alleluia! Alleluia! May the light which Thou dost send
Fill our songs with alleluias, Alleluias without end!

Approaching This Study

Open the session with a brief class activity. Ask participants to imagine that your church needs to find a new pastor. They have been appointed to a "search" committee that will write a job description for the new pastor. This description will consist of 10 "qualifications" they feel are required for the position. Together with the class, build such a list on the board or a sheet of newsprint. (Now comes the more difficult part.) Tell the class that, after much searching, they have discovered that their list is unrealistic; nobody seems to fit those qualifications. Their next task is to narrow the list down to five qualifications-and to list these in order of priority.

Once you've completed this task (try to move as quickly as possible— there may be considerable discussion), let participants explain their reasons for selecting the top three qualifications. Keep the list for discussion later in the session.

Then have participants answer the question in the Study Guide. Accept all responses. Allow time for volunteers to share their list, their ranking of the list, and the reasons for their ranking of each item.

How do the individual statements compare with the class list of qualifications for a pastor? Encourage participants to keep these activities in mind as they study Paul's comments about ministry in today's section of Colossians.

An Overview

Unit Reading

As directed in the Study Guide, participants should read **Col. 1:24–2:5** silently, underlining words or phrases used to describe Paul's role as minister and circling words or phrases that apply to all Christians. Paul was called to reveal, "the mystery that has been kept hidden . . ." "[All Christians] proclaim Him, admonishing and teaching everyone with all wisdom . . ."

The Message in Brief

Read this summary paragraph in the Study Guide aloud, inviting participants to elaborate or clarify any discoveries they made as they read the text.

Working with the Text

Work together with the entire class or allow participants to work in small groups to read and answer questions in this section of the Study Guide. If you choose to let them work in groups, you might divide the class into three groups and assign one of the subheads—"Paul's ministry of Suffering,"

"Paul's Ministry of the Word," and "The Point of the Struggle"—to each group. Then call the entire class together to share discoveries.

Paul's Ministry of Suffering (Colossians 1:24)

1. Probably the most obvious kind of suffering is imprisonment. Paul was likely under Roman house arrest because of his teachings. Encourage participants to suggest other kinds of suffering that could come from his work as a minister of the Gospel-ridicule, hatred, ostracism; anxiety and sleepless nights; disappointments when his message seemed to have no effect; discouragement when he saw Christians slipping back into sinful lives, etc. Is this kind of suffering unique to Paul, or is it something every Christian can expect?

2. Again let participants speculate. In these verses, Paul clearly sees suffering as a validation of his ministry and a sign of his authority. Ask, **Have you ever experienced joy over hardships that resulted from the Gospel? How can such suffering bolster our courage and faith in Jesus? How can it assure and affirm us in our efforts for Jesus? How can suffering put us in touch with countless other Christians—of all times and places? How might it deepen our under- standing of others and make us more effective in working with them? It is unlikely that any person who shares Jesus can escape suffering.**

Paul's Ministry of the Word (Colossians 1:25–2:1)

1. Paul defines the "glorious riches of this mystery" as "Christ in you, the hope of glory." The undeserved love which prompted God to rescue us from sin through Jesus is and always will be a mystery—a marvelous mystery. Who would expect a God who was this loving and caring? Who could believe that God would become a human being in order to suffer and die for the sins that separated us from Him? A wonderful mystery indeed! Imagine how the Colossians' awe and joy would be heightened by hearing the Gospel expressed in such thrilling terms!

2. The power for Paul's struggle and all Christians comes from Christ— "all his energy, which so powerfully works in me." Paul's frequent references to his struggles, to his suffering, to the many trials he endured, can create both respect for him as a leader who understood what he was asking of others, and an awareness of his humanity. Co-workers in Paul's ministry—pastors, leaders, and lay people today—also can expect their lives to be filled with struggle and hardships; but, as evidenced in Paul, they can also expect the wonderful strength of Christ to sustain and renew them.

The Point of the Struggle (Colossians 2:2–5)

All three aspects of ministry are tightly bound together: a proper under- standing of the mysteries of Christ will keep Christians free from error and stable in faith. The verses point out the importance of solid grounding in and understanding of the Christian Gospel. They also highlight the importance of Christian education. You might briefly discuss the responsibility all of us have to hear the truth in Jesus Christ and tell it to others.

Applying the Message

On the Larger Scene

If there is time, let individuals or small groups read and answer the questions in this section before discussing them with the entire class. If time is short, simply discuss one or both questions with the entire class. Invite your pastor to discuss his office and role within the congregation.

1. Ministers are obligated to assure that the people they serve are carefully and accurately taught the Word of God and to administer the sacraments. They are also obligated to see that the Gospel is practiced.

2. Let participants suggest answers for this question. Our society has all but lost respect for positions of authority; often, we belittle and harass leaders simply because they are leaders. As ministers of the Gospel, pastors deserve respect, love, prayers, and loyalty. Christ commanded all people, pastors and laity, to tell *all* of His love for them.

On a More Personal Level

Again, this section may be completed individually or in small groups before the whole class discusses each.

1. Encourage open discussion of this question. There are no "correct" answers, but it will be instructive to clarify participants' experiences and attitudes in the light of Paul's discussion of his suffering for the Gospel.

2. Be sure participants understand that suffering in and of itself is not a blessing. God does not will that anyone suffer-for any reason. But suffering can be transformed into a blessing by God's powerful love and presence. When it creates new understandings about others, when it leads us to a closer dependence on God, and when it enables us to identify and communicate with suffering people, God can transform suffering into blessings.

3. Again, this question should prompt open discussion about partnership between pastor and people in the ministry of your congregation. Invite the pastor to participate in this discussion. Encourage participants to suggest specific duties that might be delegated to lay people, under the guidance of the pastor. Talk about how such duties could enrich the spiritual lives of those within the congregation and community.

Taking the Lesson Home

Encourage participants to complete the Review activity, the Looking Ahead activity, and one or more of the Working Ahead suggestions before the next session. If time remains, let individuals share discoveries from last week's homework.

Closing Worship

If your pastor was able to sit in for the final part of this session, invite him to close with a brief prayer for the congregation.

Ask several volunteers to offer a prayer for the pastor and his ministry in your congregation. Then pray aloud stanzas 3 and 4 of "Thy Strong Word":

Thy strong Word bespeaks us righteous;
Bright with Thine own holiness,
Glorious now, we press toward glory,
And our lives our hopes confess.
Alleluia! Alleluia! Praise to Thee who light dost send!
Alleluia! Alleluia! Alleluia without end!

From the cross Thy wisdom shining
Breaketh forth in conqu'ring might;
From the cross forever beameth
All Thy bright redeeming light.
Alleluia! Alleluia! Praise to Thee who light dost send!
Alleluia! Alleluia! Alleluia without end!

Lesson 5

Putting Down Roots (Colossians 2:6–15)

Lesson Aim

Through His gift of faith deeply rooted in Christ, God grants His followers full, rich lives, the gift of forgiveness for times when they fail, and the faith strengthening power that enables them to serve Him in thankfulness and praise.

Lesson Objectives

By the power of the Holy Spirit working through God's Word, the participants will

1. explore the concept of "putting down roots" and list some ways in which people today look for security or roots;

2. describe Paul's beautiful advice about being rooted and growing in Christ and the fullness of life that He brings;

3. identify and evaluate some philosophies that pretend to offer roots and security to people in today's world;

4. consider ways to deepen their roots in Christian faith and to more fully experience the blessings that such commitment brings.

Opening Worship

Pray:

Heavenly Father, we thank You for the gift of Christian pastors, teachers, and dedicated lay people. Most of all, we thank You for the blessings that come as we study Your Word. Give us strength when we are weak and fail to serve You as You desire. Assure us of the forgiveness that Christ has won for us. Renew our enthusiasm and joyfulness. And show us how to sink our roots deeply in Christ, how to grow stronger and more certain in our trust in You. We know that You have promised to hear and answer us for Jesus' sake. Amen.

Approaching This Study

Open the class with discussion of "roots" and "putting down roots. Write the word "ROOTS" on the chalkboard or a large sheet of newsprint Ask participants to describe what they think of when they see or hear this word. "Roots" brings to mind images of strength, solidity, heritage. Americans have shown renewed interest in discovering and celebrating family and national roots. What accounts for this renewal?

What does it mean to "put down roots"? How do class members feel about the importance of building a sense of "grounded-ness" or stability into their lives? Is this a universal need, or is this something peculiar to our time and place? Ask participants to describe some ways in which people (themselves included) go about "putting down roots"—family, home, community, etc.

Then direct participants to the Study Guide and read the opening two paragraphs together. Today's Bible study will examine Paul's advice to the Colossian Christians about putting down roots. Give class members time to complete independently the activity describing their own roots. Then invite open sharing and discussion of their responses.

117

An Overview

Unit Reading

Have several volunteers read **Col. 2:6–15** aloud, paragraph by paragraph.

The Message in Brief

Read this paragraph aloud.

Working with the Text

Again, work through this section with the entire class or let participants work in small groups to read and answer the questions. If you choose to let them work in groups, you might divide the class into three groups, assigning each one of the subheads: "Rooted in Christ," "Empty and Deceptive Philosophy," and "Alive in Christ." Then call the groups together to discuss the entire section.

Rooted in Christ (Colossians 2:6–7)

This confession is a very clear, specific statement of faith in Jesus. When we-or any Christians-confess Jesus as Christ, Savior, and Lord, we express what we believe about Him. By saying that Jesus is the Christ, we acknowledge Him to be the Messiah whom God promised to send to rescue the world from sin. By calling Jesus "Savior," we confess that He is the one who, by His death and resurrection, has rescued us from the punishment for our sins. And by calling Jesus "Lord," we are saying that He is God, the one to whom we owe faithfulness and service. People who confess these words label themselves "Christians"—followers of Jesus. Their words and lives will bear witness to their allegiance to Jesus.

Being "rooted and built up in" Christ means that Christians draw their very lives from the power and love that Christ gives them. Their thoughts, words, actions, all spring from the source of love that Christ gives them. It's important to note that, again, this "rooted-ness" is not something that we are responsible for; God plants these roots in us and helps them to grow and demonstrate themselves ("bear fruit") in our lives as His Spirit works through Word and Sacrament. The promise of God and the knowledge of other Christians' prayers should give us confidence and hope, even in times of doubt and temptation. Our success in clinging to Christ does not depend on our determination, nor on our goodness, nor on our intention. The surety of our place in His kingdom comes only from Him.

Empty and Deceptive Philosophy (Colossians 2:8–9)

1. You might want to review the heresies that were prevalent in Paul's time—especially those that denied or confused the person and work of Jesus.

The words "take you captive" are a startling reminder of the one who inspires temptation, and who seeks to capture God's people—Satan.

2. Christians confess Jesus as Lord of all their lives. There is no room for other allegiances. These Christians were at a distinct disadvantage in Colosse. Their neighbors and possibly members of their family or friends were likely caught up in the philosophical trends of the day. Also, many of these Christians had come from backgrounds in which such heresies were taught, where rituals and dietary laws had been practiced. Paul was aware of the constant struggle that such conflicts would create for their newfound faith in Christ. Let participants speculate on some of the conflicting philosophies and attitudes that threaten Christians in our world.

3. It is important, when confronted with other philosophies that seem to promise all sorts of benefits, to remember that Christ contains "the fullness of the Deity"—He can and does give us all that we need. It is also important, when threatened by conflicting attitudes about Jesus, that the Christian recall and be assured that Jesus is truly God.

Alive in Christ (Colossians 2:10–15)

1. If Christ is the fullness of God, and Christians have been given fullness in Christ, then the Colossian Christians (and all Christians) have also received the fullness of God. Think of the incredible power of this gift! Let participants express what this gift means to the lives of Christians, the promise it offers them. This "fullness" means that we can lead truly joyful, meaningful lives, full of all the good that God wants for us. Invite speculation on what this means in terms of our happiness, our love, our friendships, our work, our worries, our hopes, etc. This is life as God intends it to be-as we would want it to be. Briefly discuss ways in which we deny our life and rebind ourselves to servitude to self and to our fears.

2. Review circumcision in **Gen. 17:9–14**, especially its spiritual aspects. Clearly, the Old Testament taught that circumcision set people apart as God's chosen and made them priests of His grace and goodness. Compare that to our place as God's people through Baptism. Why was the comparison with circumcision which was considered essential to God's Old Testament people so important?

3. Paul uses the image of "dead" in Baptism with Christ. We are dead to sin-to everything that says "self" and "fear" and "slavery," and alive to Christ and the new, holy life He gives us. Forgiveness is always the important foundation of this new Christian life. Without it we are lost indeed. We cannot make it on our own; even our best efforts to please God fail. Discuss the importance of daily repentance, forgiveness, and renewal in the rich, full life that Christ gives us.

Applying the Message

On the Larger Scene

Encourage everyone to suggest philosophies that entice modern people. On one level, there is the call of materialism—consumerism, profession, success in the job market, etc. Let participants list the promises of such a philosophy. Also discuss some of the more recent bids for loyalty by more spiritual philosophies—Eastern religions, humanism (in its various forms), new-age spiritualism, even cultic offshoots of Christianity. Encourage class members to talk about their own knowledge of and experience with these various philosophies. How does each try to fill the void—answer the universal need—of humans in our world?

On a More Personal Level

It would probably be best to allow time for participants to complete these questions independently and then, if they are willing, share and discuss their answers with the entire class.

1. As participants suggest ideas, list these on the board or a sheet of newsprint for later reference. The list might include church attendance, Bible study, Bible reading, prayer, discussion with other Christians, church activities and projects, and many more. Examine each of the suggestions for specific ways to turn each into a more effective "root-building" activity. How can "going to church" be more than just a habit or custom? What is a good way to approach devotion and Bible reading?

2. Let class members suggest ways in which a firm foundation in Christ can help in on-the-job joys and difficulties, in relationships with family and friends, etc.

3. This question calls for personal experiences. Encourage open sharing and discussion. Be sure to add your own experiences and observations to the class discussion. You might want to have the group consider the following: Do you think the experiences or "full lives" of Christians are any different in content or substance from those of non-Christians? Is it the attitude and manner in which the Christians live that makes their lives "full and rich"?

Taking the Lesson Home

Encourage participants to complete the Review activity, the Looking Ahead activity, and one or more of the Working Ahead suggestions before the next session. If time remains, let individuals share discoveries or observations from last week's suggested activities.

Closing Worship

Invite one or two volunteers to read aloud as a closing prayer the four stanzas of "How Firm a Foundation."

How firm a foundation, O saints of the Lord,
Is laid for your faith in His excellent Word!
What more can He say than to you He has said
Who unto the Savior for refuge have fled?

Fear not, I am with you, oh, be not dismayed,
For I am your God and will still give you aid;
I'll strengthen you, help you, and cause you to stand,
Upheld by My righteous, omnipotent hand.

When through fiery trials your pathway will lie,
My grace, all-sufficient, will be your supply.
The flames will not hurt you; I only design
Your dross to consume and your gold to refine.

Throughout all their lifetime My people shall prove
My sov'reign, eternal, unchangeable love;
And then, when gray hairs will their temples adorn,
Like lambs they will still in My bosom be borne.

Lesson 6

Shadow and Reality, Slavery and Freedom
(Colossians 2:16–23)

Lesson Aim

Christ provides all that we need. We need never look to other spiritual powers or intermediaries, because Christ is far greater. No religious rules or rituals can give us more than we already have. Old Testament practices are no more than a shadow of the reality—which is Christ. We depend totally on Him, not on ourselves, our efforts, nor our spirituality.

Lesson Objectives

By the power of the Holy Spirit working through God's Word, the participants will

1. examine their attitudes toward rules and regulations;

2. study and discuss Paul's words about the freedom from rules and regulations that Christ gives;

3. express in their own words the new life that Christ empowers them to live;

4. describe how Christ's forgiveness enables them to live lives of freedom in His service.

Opening Worship

Read aloud **Col. 2:1–15** to summarize the previous session. If possible, you might want to read from a different translation, such as the *New English Bible* or *Good News for Modern Man*; or else choose a paraphrased version, such as *The Living Bible*.

Approaching This Study

Read the opening paragraphs.

An Overview

Unit Reading

Ask a volunteer to read aloud **Col. 2:13–23**. Pause at the end of **verse 15** to point out the transitional word "therefore1'-which leads into the material covered in today's lesson. The two sections are closely tied together, and it is important that the group review what Paul had said previously.

The Message in Brief

Read this brief summary of **Col. 2:16–23**, inviting any comments or questions from participants.

Working with the Text

Make sure participants understand *legalism,* since it is referred to throughout this lesson. Legalism is an undue concern for and a compulsion to make and keep laws—as though keeping laws somehow makes or keeps a person holy in God's sight.

Then work though this section with the entire class, or let participants work in small groups to read and answer the six questions covered under the two subheads. If you choose to let them work in groups, you might divide participants into six teams, assigning one question to each team.

When groups have finished answering their questions, call them together to discuss the entire section.

Legalism and Slavery (Colossians 2:16–19)

1. You might want to have participants read some of the rules and regulations listed in **Leviticus 11** and **23**. These laws served both as guidelines to health and as marks that set aside the Israelites as special, chosen people of God. Many of the regulations regarding the observance of festivals were also meant to remind God's people of God's mighty acts for them and their relationship to Him. The rules were good and helpful. Paul calls these Old Testament ceremonial laws "a shadow of things to come." Such laws were no longer necessary. All that *was* necessary was faith in Christ.

2. Help participants see how the imposition of artificial rules and self-denial is really a denial of Christ and His sufficiency for us. The danger is that we will begin to trust in our *doing* instead of in Christ. It is the trap of the hypocrite, the person who feels self-important, self-sufficient, who says "I am Christian because I am good." Rather, we are Christians—God's children—through faith in Jesus and live to serve Him.

3. Old Testament regulations were, as stated earlier, meant to help God's people understand more clearly the God who had so richly loved and blessed them, and to clarify their relationship with Him. In Christ, God offers the clearest picture of what He is like and demonstrates His loving relationship with humans. Christ provides a solid, flesh-and-blood image of God. Because of Christ's perfect obedience to God's laws—even to the extent of innocently suffering death for their failure to obey the laws—His followers no longer needed to feel bound to follow ceremonial law. They had only to trust in Christ and His sacrifice for them. It would certainly be acceptable for the Christians to continue observing rules and regulations, or practice self-denial if this helped strengthen their relationship with Christ—as *long as they did not feel that these practices were somehow earning them righteousness before God.* However, they were being urged to observe the rules and practices in order to somehow qualify as Christians. It is this fallacy that Paul is speaking out against.

Freedom in Christ (Colossians 2:20–23)

1. Christians are "dead to the world" in the sense that they are no longer tied to the cares, worries, self-absorption, that drive and direct non-Christians. They no longer need to feel trapped and enslaved by the compulsive need to "achieve" or "succeed" in order to prove themselves and their worth. Christ has, by His work, *made them worthy.* This is freedom. Encourage participants to describe the difference this knowledge and

understanding would make in one's approach to a job, home, wealth, entertainment, and friends.

2. These "taboos" involved restrictions and regulations on foods and other items that were considered "clean" and "unclean." ("Do not handle! Do not taste!") Practices such as voluntarily denying oneself certain foods or activities—for example, during Lent or on special days (let participants suggest other examples)—can enrich a Christian's life, if such denial serves as a reminder of Christ's sacrifice. Danger arises when we think of such practices as means through which we can earn God's favor or make ourselves better in His sight.

3. Paul is saying that legalistic regulations result in three things: *apparent* humility, *apparent* wisdom, and *actual* self-indulgence. Others may be impressed by such actions ("She must really be a good person," "He must really believe what he preaches," etc.), but this is merely outward impressions; a "good show." Ask participants to talk about how such practices can actually be a form of self-indulgence—even as they appear to curb such indulgence. How is rigorous self-denial often a method of pampering oneself, of drawing attention to oneself, of saying to oneself and others, "Look how good I am?" It is only when these practices stem from a true sense of and gratitude for the gift Christ has won for us that they can be helpful and meaningful. Of themselves, these actions cannot make us better persons or more worthy in God's sight.

Applying the Message

On the Larger Scene

These questions could first be discussed and answered in small groups and then shared with the entire class. Or, if time is short, you might want to read and discuss the questions with the whole class.

1. Encourage participants to describe forms of slavery—both spiritual and secular—that attract Christians in today's world. On the secular level, there is the temptation to surrender your life to the pursuit of material things, to scaling a corporate ladder, to having the "ideal" family, the "best" marriage, or to the pursuit of pleasures all at the expense of your relationship with Jesus. Forms of spiritual slavery are just as real today as they were in Paul's time. Consider Christians who join sects, cults, or a church that teaches contrary to God's Word. Let class members provide specific examples, if possible. How are such attractions really forms of slavery?

2. Let class members speculate on the appeal of such demands. What causes people to respond eagerly to rules, regulations, and demands of their time, money, and lives? Which seems easier-to pray God's Word for direction in our lives, or to let leaders tell us how to act, what to say, how to feel? Is the desire to somehow *make ourselves* better people—to work out

our own salvation—any different from the motives that drove the misguided people of Paul's time?

3. The danger in any submission is the likelihood we will begin to feel *we* are able to make ourselves better, that *we* can please God by our efforts. It just isn't true. Only by God's grace, by the gift of His Son, are we made better; and this is something that has already been done for us. The other danger in submitting to legalism is that we will become mindless automatons, willingly serving and obeying leaders without thinking or wrestling for Christ's guidance and power in our choices.

On a More Personal Level

Each of these questions calls for a personal response. Allow participants time to think about and then write their answers. Then invite—but don't force—open sharing and discussion with the entire class. There are obviously no "correct" answers; the following suggestions are meant to serve only as guides and discussion starters.

1. Answers will vary from person to person. Let participants consider the seeming paradox in "servants" who are "truly free." How is service to Jesus a form of freedom that enables us to discover what life is really meant to be? How does it free us from cares and concerns about earthly matters?

2. Again, let participants discuss this from their own experiences with freedom. What roadblocks often turn us aside and often drive us back to slavery? How does freedom in Christ involve effort and struggle to seek His direction? Is this sort of struggle true of any kind of real freedom? Invite examples and thoughts from participants.

3. A Christian's freedom is limited or directed by a genuine concern and love for others, and by the desire to reach out to others with the Good News of Christ. Let participants describe ways in which those concerns might focus or direct their own freedom regarding observance of rules or talking with people who are caught up in such observances. Why is freedom in Christ always concerned about other people?

Taking the Lesson Home

Encourage participants to complete the Review activity, the Looking Ahead activity, and one or more of the Working Ahead suggestions before the next session.

Closing Worship

Read the following excerpts from **Gal. 5:1–6.**

It is for freedom that Christ has set us free. Stand firm, then, and do not let yourselves be burdened again by a yoke of slavery. Mark my words! ...You who are trying to be justified by law have been alienated from Christ; you have fallen away from grace. But by faith we eagerly await through the Spirit the righteousness for which we hope. . . . The only thing that counts is faith expressing itself through love.

Then close by thanking God for the wonderful gift of freedom and asking for the wisdom and power to express that freedom in love and concern for one another.

Lesson 7

New Life-What It Is Not (Colossians 3:1–11)

Lesson Aim

Through the free gift of God in Baptism, we are changed in a wonderful way—our sinful natures are put to death, and the spirit and power of Christ live in us. With Christ living in us, our lives are changed, and we are enabled to show our faith by words and deeds of love and kindness. However, this remarkable change is an ongoing, daily process; and because we are human, we will often fail to live as new creatures. We have God's assurance of forgiveness for those times when we fail, and we have His promise to be with us always and empower us to live for Him once more.

Lesson Objectives

By the power of the Holy Spirit working through God's Word, the participants will

1. describe the process of change and new life that God works in Christians;

2. apply Paul's description of the "old life" and the "new life in Christ" to their own experiences and struggles with faith;

3. confess their failures to forsake their old, sinful natures, and affirm the power of Christ's forgiveness to restore and renew them as holy, "set-apart" people.

Opening Worship

Read aloud **Col. 2:13–14**. As an opening prayer, read stanzas 1–3 and 5 of "In Adam We Have All Been One."

In Adam we have all been one,
One huge rebellious man;
We all have fled that evening voice
That sought us as we ran.

We fled our God, and, fleeing Him,
We lost our brother too;
Each singly sought and claimed His own;
Each man his brother slew.

But Your strong love, it sought us still
And sent Your only Son
That we might hear His shepherd's voice
And, hearing Him, be one.

Send us Your Spirit, teach us truth
To purge our vanity;
From fancied wisdom, self-sought ways,
O Savior, set us free.

Approaching This Study

Read aloud the brief paragraph of instructions in the Study Guide. Assure the participants that the first part of this section—the listing of changes—will be completely confidential. However, the questions following this listing will be discussed by the group. Allow time for everyone to complete the survey and answer the questions.

Discuss the questions that follow together with the entire class. Did anyone have trouble coming up with two changes? How many have ever seriously wished they could change things about themselves? When and why do such thoughts occur? Do they think this desire to change is common to most people? Why do people so often want to change themselves? What's behind such longing? Note how the survey was phrased-and how the desire is often expressed: "If I *could* change . . ." Is such change possible? Have participants ever tried? Briefly discuss the enormous sums of money spent on counseling, psychoanalysis, therapy, etc.

Explain that this lesson will explore the question of change.

An Overview

Unit Reading

Read the paragraph in the Study Guide. Then ask one or two volunteers to read aloud Paul's words in **Col. 3:1–11**. After the reading, let participants describe how Paul explains Christianity in exclusive terms-by what it is not.

The Message in Brief

Read this explanatory paragraph aloud. Note how, once again, it is important to keep in mind what has preceded this section of the letter. Paul carefully builds his case, and he will often refer to earlier words as preparation for what will come next.

Working with the Text

You may choose to allow time for individuals to read and answer questions under this section and then discuss it with the entire class. Or let participants work in small groups to read and answer the questions. If you work in groups, you could divide the class into three groups and assign one subhead to each group: "Motive and Power for Change;" "Killing the 'Old Life;'" and "Taking on the New Life."

Motive and Power for Change (Colossians 3:1–4)

1. Through faith in Christ—a gift we receive through Baptism—we receive Christ's spirit and power. It is exactly as if we are reborn, as if we come to life—real, full life. Christ gives us power over sin and death. This is the gift that God gives every Christian.

2. The biblical term "right hand designated a position of power. Christ is in the position of power with God. This assurance of Christ's divine status is wonderful comfort and assurance for Christians. We can change into new, better beings, through faith strengthened as the Holy Spirit works through God's Word, God promises to change us.

3. Christians' sights are figuratively and literally "set higher"—on things of heaven. Our sights are set on the goal of our new lives—being with Christ eternally. Think how this goal can free us from worldly cares and striving while, at the same time, enabling us to enjoy our lives on earth. In connection with this concept, you might want to talk about the sense in which all Christians are "holy." Our motive to live the Christian life is not an attempt to be holy or to achieve some measure of goodness that approaches holiness. We are holy because Christ makes us holy, and we live a life of dedication and service in response to His goodness and grace.

Killing the "Old Life" (Colossians 3:5–9)

1. The "old life" or "earthly nature" refers to our state before receiving the gift of faith in Christ-our condition of sinfulness and our bondage to things of this world. Christians need to shed this old life, to eliminate it from their new condition as children of God. Let participants suggest ways in which this "putting to death" needs to take place daily.

2. Participants may list such sins as sexual promiscuity or perversions or obsessions, lust, greed, envy, anger, rage, hatred, lying, cursing, and foul language. You needn't spend a lot of time listing the sins that are to be absent from the Christian life. However, it might be interesting to have participants compare the list here with the ones in **Eph. 4:31** and **Gal. 5:19–21**. Talk about the similarities and differences. What things are often repeated?

3. As was discussed earlier, Christians are also human; and, as such, are continually tempted to turn back to their old lives. This process of change, which is empowered by Christ, involves daily repentance and forgiveness.

4. In discussing this question, you might want to make sure participants understand God's attitude toward sin. Sometimes we are tempted to soft pedal His wrath and assume that in some mysterious way God will overlook our sin or excuse it. As difficult as this might be, we must affirm with Paul that God condemns and punishes sin. If He does not, what is the purpose of Christ's death? God still condemns sin, but He loves sinners and offers free salvation to all sinners through faith in Jesus Christ.

Taking on the New Life (Colossians 3:10–11)

1. When God created the first people, He made them in His own image— sinless and holy. Because of their sin, people lost God's image. Christ was the "second Adam"—He, too, was holy and without sin. Christ never lost God's image. When Christians are filled with Christ's spirit and power- when they are born again-through Holy Baptism they are given the image of God. Through the forgiveness which Christ won for them, and which God offers them, their sins are washed away. They are made holy and sinless in God's sight. Again, it is good to remind participants that the process of forgiveness and renewal must be a continual, daily part of the Christian life.

2. When people are born again through faith in Christ, they are changed. Each of them bears the image of God; each is powered and motivated by Christ's Spirit. In their essence, they are all alike; differences such as race, sex, nationality, etc, no longer matter.

Applying the Message

On the Larger Scene

You may want to assign these questions for small group discussion before covering them with the entire class. Or, if time is short, you could read and discuss the questions with everyone.

1. Most likely, participants will suggest that all the sins bear mentioning to Christians today. Certainly they are all evident in newspaper and television reports daily. Christians today are susceptible to and involved in such sins.

2. There are no easy answers to this question. A Christian demonstrates faith through words and actions, through love and concern for others, and through efforts to spread the Good News about Jesus. But it is not for us to determine or judge just how often, where, and in what form such demonstrations of faith are to show themselves. If a Christian's life demonstrates nothing but obvious signs of the old life—sins such as those mentioned in Paul's letter—it is our responsibility to confront him or her in love. Let participants suggest ways of approaching such people with firmness but genuine love for them.

3. Encourage participants to express ideas in their own words, drawing from their own experiences and those of people they know. The longing to change most probably stems from the old life—sin—that is in all of us. We sense somehow that we could, *should*, be better people: happier, kinder, more self-controlled, more concerned about others, closer to God. Do class members sense God's Spirit active in such longing? If so, how? What obligation do we have to such people—as people who *have* experienced change (even if we're still not where we want to be in the process)?

4. Let participants respond to this question. A basic change of character, from evil to holy (and that is *one major change*!) is basic to the Christian faith. What wonderful promise does Christianity hold for people desperate to become "better"? Ask class members how a Christian might approach such people with the Good News of the Gospel. How would Christians explain the concept of becoming "better people"?

On a More Personal Level

Both questions in this section call for very personal answers-ones that participants may wish not to share with others. Be sure to honor any such wishes in your class discussion. It may be helpful if you lead off with thoughts and observations of your own (if you're willing).

Allow time for participants individually to think about the questions and make notes. Then ask for volunteers to open the discussion.

1. Most often, we cling to "favorite" sins or bad habits out of a false sense of security. We've grown used to them. We know what they're like. We feel momentary thrills when practicing them. How can a knowledge of Christ's power help? How might prayer? How can other Christians provide support and assurance and *courage*? Let participants offer as many specific, concrete suggestions and illustrations as possible.

2. Such attitudes are probably more common than we'd like to believe. Attitudes like these are closely related to the situation described in question 1: we don't want to give up certain sins *just yet*, feeling confident that we'll always be able to get forgiveness and change later—before it's too late. What does such an attitude say about our commitment to our faith? To our willingness to surrender and let Christ work in us?

You might want to recall the earlier discussion about God's attitude toward sin. If God does not strongly condemn sin, what is the purpose of Christ's death for sin? He loves sinners (that's why He sent Jesus; that's why He offers us the power of Jesus for change), but also expects perfection of His people.

Taking the Lesson Home

Encourage participants to complete the Review activity, the Looking Ahead activity, and one or more of the Working Ahead suggestions before the next session. If time remains, ask participants to share discoveries from previous "Working Ahead activities.

Closing Worship

Read again **Col. 3:1–11**. Then pray stanzas 1–3 of "Eternal Spirit of the Living Christ".

Eternal Spirit of the living Christ,
I know not how to ask or what to say;
I only know my need, as deep as life,
And only You can teach me how to pray.

Come, pray in me the prayer I need this day;
Help me to see Your purpose and Your will,
Where I have failed, what I have done amiss;
Held in forgiving love, let me be still.

Come with the strength I lack, bring vision clear
Of human need; oh, give me eyes to see
Fulfillment of my life in love outpoured;
My life in You, O Christ; Your love in me. Amen.

Lesson 8

New Life—What It Is (Colossians 3:12–17)

Lesson Aim

Through God's gift of faith, we are changed into new creatures. With the power of Christ's Spirit living and working in us, we reflect God's love and forgiveness in our relationships with others. We also have God's promise of forgiveness and renewal for those times when we fail to reflect Christ living in us.

Lesson Objectives

By the power of the Holy Spirit working through God's Word, the participants will

1. describe characteristics that define Christian faith in action;

2. discuss and define Paul's description of virtues that flow from faith in Christ;

3. name specific ways in which Christians today—themselves included—can give evidence to their Christian faith;

4. thank God for the power of Christ in their own lives and pray for increased strength to let that power direct their attitudes, words, and actions.

Opening Worship

Pray stanzas 1–3 of "Renew Me, O Eternal Light".

Renew me, O eternal Light,
And let my heart and soul be bright,
Illumined with the light of grace
That issues from Your holy face.

Remove the pow'r of sin from me
And cleanse all my impurity
That I may have the strength and will
Temptations of the flesh to still.

Create in me a new heart, Lord,
That gladly I obey Your Word.
Let what You will be my desire,
And with new life my soul inspire.

Approaching This Study

Direct participants to the Study Guide and read the opening paragraph with them. Then divide the class into groups of two or three people. Let the groups discuss ideas and then complete the list of five characteristics that demonstrate Christian faith.

Call the class back together to share lists. Note on the board or newsprint those characteristics that are repeated by the groups, and invite each group to explain briefly the reasons for the choices. Are these traits unique to Christians? What difference is there between a Christian who is, say, "generous," and a non-Christian who also shows generosity? Keep your board list handy for reference and comparison as you discuss Paul's words about the new life in Christ.

An Overview

Unit Reading

Read aloud the Study Guide paragraph and then ask for several volunteers to read **Col. 3:12–17**. You may want to let participants quickly review the previous session's material, describing what the new life is *not*, as a lead-in to the discussion of these verses.

The Message in Brief

Read this summary paragraph aloud to the group and invite reactions and comments. Help the group see how beautifully the letter to the Colossians builds on itself. Paul is not only equipping these Christians to deal with challenges to their faith, he is also carefully instructing them in the basics of Christian life.

Working with the Text

Consider varying your approach to this section of the Study Guide. If you've been working with small groups in previous sessions, you might want to make this a whole-class activity this week, or vice-versa. Allow time for participants to read and answer the questions individually before discussing each.

A Life of Forgiveness (Colossians 3:12–13)

1. With phrases such as these, Paul directed the Christians to the great gift of God's love—a wonderful reassurance and source of comfort, and a reminder of the power that is theirs for the taking. These reminders should have made the Colossians willing and eager to hear Paul's instructions, and instilled confidence that they could carry out those instructions—with God's

help. Let participants respond to being described as "God's chosen people, holy and dearly loved."

2. Let participants compare their lists and definitions with those of other members of the class. Here are some guidelines from a dictionary: Compassionate: sympathetic awareness of others' distress together with a desire to alleviate it; Kind: affectionate, loving; Humble: not proud or haughty; Gentle: mild-mannered and kind; Patient: steadfast and true, despite opposition or difficulty.

3. It is only through the forgiveness which we have in Christ—and which we can then show to others—that we are able to demonstrate compassion, kindness, humility, gentleness, and patience. Knowing that we are forgiven, despite our sins and shortcomings and our own sense of worthlessness, we can gratefully share that forgiveness with other sinful humans through words and actions of compassion, kindness, etc.

A Life of Love and Peace (Colossians 3:14–15)

1. Encourage participants to describe contemporary ideas about love— romantic love, friendship, parental love, etc., and compare these with the description of *agape*. No matter how good or noble earthly love seems, it is always sullied by self-concern; it always involves some kind of reciprocation—we want something in return for our love. Not so with divine love, the love inspired by and originating from God. Christians have tasted this love as they experience God's love and forgiveness for them in Christ. To the extent that they can themselves demonstrate this kind of love, Christians are indebted to Christ—who supplies them with such love. However, this process of showing Christian love is a continual, daily struggle. We need constantly to draw on Christ's love and forgiveness as our power source. Let participants describe how the assurance that *we* are loved unconditionally enables them to demonstrate similar love in their lives.

2. The "peace of Christ" stems from the love of Christ. This peace is not the absence of all conflict, nor is it ease and comfort. It is the powerful assurance of God's unswerving love for us in Jesus that permits us to live at peace with Him—and then, also, at peace with ourselves and with others.

A Life of Worship and Thanksgiving (Colossians 3:16–17)

1.**Verse 16** describes worship as letting "the word of Christ dwell in you richly" (again, the knowledge of God's love and mighty act of redemption) and, with that as a basis, teaching and admonishing one another (Christians) with all wisdom, and singing "psalms, hymns and spiritual songs with gratitude in your hearts to God." Let participants relate how this definition of worship compares with their own experiences and ideas. Kinds and styles of worship vary-but worship must always center in Jesus Christ and the good news of His forgiveness.

2. Connect this discussion with the earlier description of worship. Help participants see how our lives—dedicated to Jesus, with deeds done in His name—become a kind of thankful worship. It is only in the name of Jesus, because of what He has done for us, and by His power in us, that we can worship—or live new lives. This is the motive and power for our thanksgiving.

Applying the Message

On the Larger Scene

You may want to assign these questions for small group discussion before covering them with the entire class. Or, if time is short, read and discuss the questions with everyone.

1. Briefly compare Paul's list of Christian virtues with that developed by the class. Are many of the same characteristics included in both lists—but in different words?

Invite participants to share thoughts on specific ways in which Christians today can demonstrate these virtues through words and actions. Encourage the group—yourself included—to examine their own lives for such demonstrations of Christian virtues.

2. Discuss the concept of minimum standards. The trap of a minimum standard for Christian behavior is very real. In the first place, it invites judgment of others and self-righteousness. And such a standard is a trap because the minimum varies for different people. Some need God's grace to overcome mountains of inner pain and insecurity in order to accomplish any "good" at all. We all need encouragement to be less critical and more understanding of the faults and failings of others.

3. Invite participants to share names they have listed and to explain why they have chosen these Christians. It is good to have role models after which to pattern our own behavior, and it is heartening and up-building to see what Christian faith can accomplish. However, we must always remember that our role models are humans who fail and will continue to fail. If we put too much stock in humans, we're certain to be disappointed and disillusioned. The only perfect role model is Christ; we have not only His example to follow, but also His power to direct our lives.

On a More Personal Level

For these questions, it might be good to let participants work in small groups to discuss and arrive at answers. Both questions focus on very real and perplexing issues for Christians. The opportunity to share experiences and pool ideas with several other Christians could be helpful.

Both questions strike at the heart of Christian faith and growth in Christ. There are no "correct" answers to either question. Encourage participants to share ideas and experiences and to discuss these in terms of their potential effectiveness. A time of supportive sharing, and reassurance of forgiveness might be helpful to those who struggle.

We do not express forgiveness or love because *we decide* to do so, but because we recognize the greatness of God's love for us in Jesus. When we truly apprehend and feel this love in our own lives, we gain the "peace of Christ" that enables us to feel secure about ourselves. *Then* we can draw on God's power to love and forgive others.

Taking the Lesson Home

Encourage participants to complete the Review activity, the Looking Ahead activity, and one or more of the Working Ahead suggestions before the next session. If time remains in this session, ask participants to share discoveries from previous "Working Ahead activities.

Closing Worship

Read **Gal. 5:16–25**—Paul's beautiful description of the Christian life in terms of "fruit of the Spirit." Pray for God's power to live in such a way that the "fruit" of the Spirit will be evident in our own lives. Or close by praying stanza 3 of "Renew Me, O Eternal Light".

Create in me a new heart, Lord,
That gladly I obey Your Word.
Let what You will be my desire,
And with new life my soul inspire. Amen.

Lesson 9

Christians at Home and at Work
(Colossians 3:18–4:1)

Lesson Aim

Christ in His love and forgiveness—builds strong families. The love, submission, obedience, and respect expressed in Christian households reflect the love, submission, obedience, and respect demonstrated by Christ. Perhaps the most important resource on which Christian family members can draw is the gift of forgiveness which God freely offers in times when we fail to be all that He desires us to be.

Lesson Objectives

By the power of the Holy Spirit working through God's Word, the participants will

1. explore the state of the family in their world and express their own experiences with and attitudes about families;

2. restate Paul's advice to Christian families and discuss how that advice applies to families today;

3. express ways in which the assurance of Christ's love and forgiveness can positively affect relationships within their own families;

4. thank God for His forgiveness in the times when they sin against the family members, and pray for the power to offer that same forgiveness to family members who sin against them.

Opening Worship

Read **Col. 2:6–7**, Paul's beautiful encouragement to be rooted in Christ and overflowing with thankfulness. Pray:

Lord, help us sink our roots deeply in You. Fill us with Your love, Your forgiveness, Your wisdom, so that our lives demonstrate Christ living in us. Give us more compassion, kindness, humility, gentleness, and patience-so that we can more truly love ourselves as Your new people, and more fully show Your love to everyone we meet. We pray in Jesus' name. Amen.

Approaching This Study

The subject of families is not only a hot item in the news, it is also a topic fraught with strong feelings and a lot of emotional baggage for many people. Be aware that some participants may feel threatened by parts of this session, while others may use the material as a springboard for strongly felt political and personal views. Pray for God's grace and wisdom as you guide the discussions. Try to be sensitive to the emotions underlying many of the comments and challenges that arise.

Direct participants to the Study Guide and read the opening three paragraphs aloud with them. First allow several minutes for class members to recall and note their favorite childhood family memory. Encourage them to apply this memory to the next part of the activity.

Divide your class into four groups and assign one unfinished statement to each group. Allow time for groups to discuss and reach a consensus regarding the statements. Then have each group present its completed statement about the family. As the groups explain how and why they arrived at these definitions, note the statements on the chalkboard or on newsprint for later reference. Invite comments and discussion from other class members after each group has presented.

An Overview

Unit Reading

Have two volunteers read the suggested section of **Colossians**; one can read verses **3:12–17**, and the other—**3:18–4:1**.

The Message in Brief

Read this paragraph aloud to the class. Stress the importance of Paul's early words to the Colossians as a basis for the rules regarding Christian families and households.

Working with the Text

Allow independent time for participants to read this section and answer the questions under each heading. Then discuss each question with the entire class.

Wives and Husbands (Colossians 3:18–19)

Have a volunteer read the paragraph about "contemporary philosophers" aloud. Call attention to the final sentences, "Christians did not seek to change the social structure of their world. They sought rather to inject a new and higher relationship in the social order—namely, 'as is fitting in the Lord.'" Ask someone to explain what this means. Christians worked within the structure of their times, which provided a good model for outward behavior; however, they sought to provide a solid basis or motivation for the behavior—Christ's love and forgiveness. How important is this for families today?

1. According to Paul's injunction to wives, the husband was to be head of the household and wives were to submit to him. However, the phrase "in the Lord" and the fact that Paul was assuming his readers saw themselves—and one another—as "God's chosen people," cast a new light on the command. As new creatures in Christ, all members of the family would also seek to express compassion, kindness, humility, gentleness, patience, love, and forgiveness in their dealings with one another. Let participants explain how this would affect wives' relationships with their husbands, and vice versa.

While not making it the central point of discussion, you can anticipate that some in your class will want to discuss "equal rights" within the marriage, or will have questions about abusive husbands or single-parent households. These are all valid issues and worth consideration from a Christian perspective. Allow free expression and discussion of such questions. Help participants understand how the underlying foundation of Christ's love can apply to each of these situations, how it empowers single parents, and how this speaks to partners in dysfunctional homes. The basis of Christian families must be a love that engenders mutual respect and attends to the needs of parents and children.

We love as Christ loved us—self-sacrificing, expecting nothing in return, undeserved, etc.

2. As in the above question, Paul is urging a love which is based on Christ's power and on His forgiveness. This love involves compassion, kindness, humility, etc., and it will lead to mutual respect and cooperation.

Children and Parents (Colossians 3:20–2:1)

1. This discussion could easily slip into a complaining session about disrespectful and disobedient children today, and a blaming session against parents who do not sufficiently discipline or encourage their children. Paul urges a kind of obedience that springs from love—the Christ-centered love that lives in people whose lives have been changed by His grace.

Encourage participants to consider how children might practice such advice when they find themselves in difficult—even abusive—situations. What does God's love and concern for each of us say in these cases? There are no easy answers to such questions. A discussion of confession, encouragement, support, and forgiveness may be helpful.

2. Undoubtedly the father had the major responsibility for discipline in Paul's world, especially for his sons. Changing culture, life-styles, and parental roles have affected that situation in our world. Both parents are to be firm, fair, encouraging, and loving as they deal with their children.

Slaves and Masters (Colossians 3:22–4:1)

You might want to wait until lesson 13 for a lengthy discussion of slavery and its relationship to the Christian life. However, be sure participants understand that the whole issue of slavery was a troubling one to Paul, and he struggled to bring a sense of Christian love to relationships between Christian masters and servants.

1. Duties of slaves include obedience to masters, honesty, faithfulness, and hard work. The virtues Paul encourages are trustworthiness, sincerity, respect, and diligence. As in the situation with Christian families, lives and actions are motivated by faith in and dedication to Christ.

2. Masters must, above all, be just and fair in dealing with their slaves. Christian masters are themselves slaves to Christ. With Christ's love directing their lives, they not only should be just and fair; they also have the power to be so.

Ask participants to describe ways in which these words about slaves and masters can also apply to the workplace. How does the love of Christ and the qualities of compassion, kindness, humility, gentleness, patience, and forgiveness affect relationships between employer and employee?

Applying the Message

On the Larger Scene

You may want to assign these questions for small group discussion before covering them with the entire class. If time is short, read and discuss the questions with everyone. You will want to refer to the definitions and comments about families that participants completed early in the session.

1. Let participants describe and discuss the results of conditions that affect family life in our world: divorce, single-parent households, working parents, homelessness, abusive homes, pressure in the workplace (parents) and in schools (children), the threat of urban gangs, etc. Which, if any, of these, have participants experienced in their own family life? Encourage a spirit of openness and trust in which problems can be shared and solutions sought among the participants.

2. Considering those factors, and the opening discussion, how would participants define a "successful" family in today's world? There are no "correct" answers here, but it is important that participants—and the Christian church—address the Gospel message to real people in real situations. And, in order to do this, we need a firm grasp on what is happening in our world. Are these definitions different from the earlier one? If so, how and why are they different?

3. Listen to as many pieces of advice as possible. Invite discussion regarding the reasons behind this advice and the potential effects of such advice to members of the family. How is the Christian faith evident in such advice? How palatable would the advice be for non-Christian families?

What might Christians add to such advice-actions, concern, follow-up—in order to help troubled families overcome problems?

On a More Personal Level

Allow enough time for participants to complete this activity independently before discussing the questions with the class. Assure everyone that their answers for the first question need not be shared with the class.

1. If anyone is willing to share some of the "best" family experiences, allow them to do so. In what way-if at all-did faith in Christ play a part in these good experiences?

2. Again, answers will vary. Invite volunteers to share and discuss insights that might help other family members.

3. As you listen to participants' ideas about "the most important thing for Christian family members to practice," compare these with the earlier definitions from the opening activity. If it is not mentioned by anyone, be sure to add "forgiveness" to the list. Let participants describe their understanding of forgiveness—as practiced and empowered by Christ. How is forgiveness important in dysfunctional families? How can it help abused wives, husbands, and children to live with *themselves*? With their abusers (even if this means living apart from such abusers)? How can forgiveness help to heal individuals and families? Forgiveness is one of the most difficult concepts to grasp—and even more difficult to practice. We are often so caught up in our own guilt and hurt that we cannot even forgive ourselves. An understanding of grace (God truly loves and forgives me through faith in Jesus.) through ongoing study of God's Word and a strong prayer life are essential.

Taking the Lesson Home

Encourage participants to complete the Review activity, the Looking Ahead activity, and one or more of the Working Ahead suggestions before the next session. If time remains in this session, ask participants to share discoveries from previous Working Ahead activities.

Closing Worship

For a closing prayer, read aloud these stanzas of "Oh, Blest the House".
Oh, blest the house, whate'er befall,
Where Jesus Christ is all in all!
For if He were not dwelling there,
How dark and poor and void it were!

Oh, blest that house where faith is found
And all in charity abound
To trust their God and serve Him still
And do in all His holy will!

Oh, blest that house; it prospers well!
In peace and joy the parents dwell,
And in their children's lives is shown
How richly God can bless His own.

Then here will I and mine today
A solemn cov'nant make and say:
Though all the world forsake His Word,
My house and I will serve the Lord.

Lesson 10

*Always Praying and Witnessing
(Colossians 4:2–6)*

Lesson Aim

To a Christian, prayer is both a privilege and a necessity. Christ has earned the right for us to approach God, and He promises to help and strengthen us in our lives of prayer.

Lesson Objectives

By the power of the Holy Spirit working through God's Word, the participants will

1. assess their attitudes toward and practice of prayer through a brief survey and discussion;

2. develop a clear, personal definition of prayer that includes Paul's admonition to "devote yourselves to prayer" and to be "watchful and thankful;"

3. list ways in which they and other Christians can more effectively express faith in Christ to non-Christians;

4. pray for God's guidance and strength in building their own prayer practices.

Opening Worship

Pray the Lord's Prayer together with your class. Then ask for prayer suggestions from the participants—both requests and words of thanks. Either include these in a prayer that you offer, or else start with a brief prayer of your own and invite volunteers to add their own requests and thank-Yous.

Approaching This Study

Direct participants to the Study Guide and read the opening two paragraphs together. Then allow independent time for class members to answer the first two questions and complete the prayer survey provided in number 3.

Discuss the first two questions with the class. Work for a "class answer" to questions 1 and 2, and note these on the chalkboard or a sheet of newsprint. Should the definition of prayer include listening as well as speaking to God? How are thoughts and feelings a part of our prayers? In what way is our entire life—thoughts, feelings, and actions—a prayer to or communication with God? Participants should understand that prayer is a vital link with God; it is a way of seeking specific guidance for our lives, a way of making Bible truths real and personal.

In discussing the prayer survey, you will want to build an attitude of openness and acceptance. There should be no judging of attitudes, no attempts to "correct" or change feelings. With the help of God's Spirit working through God's Word, participants may find answers to some of their questions in the class discussion. Ask, "How many participants would like to improve their prayer life?"

An Overview

Unit Reading

Have a volunteer read **Col. 4:2–6** aloud, pausing after each verse.

The Message in Brief

Read the paragraph in the Study Guide with the participants. Note that Paul's final plea to the Colossian Christians is for their prayers and efforts to spread the Gospel.

Working with the Text

You might divide the class into seven small teams and assign one question from this section to each team. Or else, allow time for participants to work through all of the questions independently before discussing them with the entire class.

Prayer That Is Constant, Watchful, and Thankful (Colossians 4:2)

1. Paul did expect the Colossian Christians to take his words literally. Let participants offer suggestions about how Christians can continue daily—even hourly—in their efforts at prayer. Reflect on the opening discussion of what prayer means. If prayer involves an offering of all our thoughts and feelings to God (rather than just specific, designated time periods that we deliberately set aside to pray), this is not an unusual or difficult task. If Christians have a continual sense of Christ's presence within them—if they can remember that God is always beside and within them—then it becomes more and more natural to share everything with Him. Listening for His advice and wisdom and direction becomes a constant occupation. A major part of our problem with prayer results from a decision to compartmentalize it, to block out periods for talking with God. Once we can expand our understanding of prayer, we can begin to practice it more often and more effectively.

2. The point of this parable is that persistence in prayer pays off. Let participants describe the effect that continual communication with God will have on the person who prays. By the act of constant prayer, we assure ourselves that God is there, that He is listening, that He cares. Point out that persistence does not mean repetition, but rather steadfast efforts to reach God's answers, to hear His voice.

3. Watchfulness is every bit as important as persistence in prayer. Without it, we are not sincerely wishing God to hear us, wishing Him to answer us. The measure of our watchfulness is also the measure of our faith that God hears and answers prayer.

4. Thankfulness stems from our knowledge that prayer is a privilege, one that was bought at a very dear price Jesus' suffering and death. We can be thankful, even in the most tragic and desperate situations, that God loves us, begs us to speak with Him, and promises to hear and answer us. A spirit of thankfulness makes our prayers more real to us and fans the flames of faith in a God who hears us.

Prayer for the Gospel (Colossians 4:34)

Paul asks that the Colossians pray for his success in spreading the Good News about Jesus. We might expect that he would ask them to pray for his deliverance from prison, for an easier life, for relief from suffering. As we pray for others' success at spreading the Gospel, we affirm that the task is indeed a worthy one, that the Gospel message is of vital importance. Let participants explain what effect this would have on a Christian's own efforts to tell the Good News. How would it help Paul to know that others were praying for him?

Witnessing to the Gospel (Colossians 4:5–6)

1. Several times in his letter, Paul asks that God provide the Colossians with wisdom—the wisdom that comes from knowledge of Jesus and the faith He grants. By wise dealings with outsiders, Paul refers to interactions that will make non-Christians open to and accepting of the message about Jesus and His love for them. Encourage group members to suggest ways in which we can build such openness in the people we meet.

2. Answers will vary. Let participants offer ideas about how our words and actions can inspire trust and respect in the people we meet—trust and respect that may open their minds to the faith that we hold. Our motivation in any encounters must always be twofold: first, we act out of the love Christ has shown us (these are people whom God dearly loves); and second, we must work to build receptive attitudes to the Gospel.

Applying the Message

On the Larger Scene

It might be good to assign these questions to small groups before discussing them with the entire class. All questions call for personal opinion and interpretation, so encourage the groups to approach their discussions with open minds.

1. What do participants think about attitudes toward prayer among today's Christians? How do their answers reflect their own feelings and experiences? In fact, in recent years there has been some resurgence of interest in spiritual matters—including prayer. This resurgence has taken some rather strange and unusual directions, with an emphasis on Eastern religions, "earth" religions, "new age" groups, and cults. However, it has also reached many Christian denominations as well; and within many congregations are core groups of curious, concerned Christians who are eager to explore new spiritual depths of their faith. How is it true that lukewarm approaches often net lukewarm—or even less than lukewarm—results? Listen to and discuss suggestions for building enthusiasm for prayer. What have group members found successful in stimulating their own prayer lives?

Generally, it seems that Christians are taking a "bum rap" in much of the media reports these days. This negative attitude no doubt stems from such incidents as the Waco cult and radical activists on both sides of some controversial issues such as abortion, euthanasia, and gay rights. What is unfortunate about such coverage? What lessons can Christians learn from such media reports that might help them confess their faith in Christ more effectively?

On a More Personal Level

Allow time for participants to work through this section independently. Then discuss the questions with the entire class.

1. Rather than put anyone on the spot for this question, why not invite "suggestions" that people have found helpful in making their own prayer experiences more meaningful? List some of these on the chalkboard or a sheet of newsprint and encourage questions from group members.

2. Again invite suggestions regarding effective witnessing. Do participants feel that it is important to feel "comfortable" about witnessing? Can other people sense discomfort in such matters? And if so, what effect will this have on the effectiveness of such witnessing? Does the discussion suggest anything about our understanding of what it means to "witness"? Can anyone offer a clear, acceptable definition of "witness" that might help? What might a feeling of discomfort indicate about our conviction regarding our own faith? Could there be a prior step—before talking to others about our faith—that we might want to concentrate on in order to gain a stronger sense of conviction in our own faith? How can prayer be an essential part of such a step?

Taking the Lesson Home

Encourage participants to complete the Review activity, the Looking Ahead activity, and one or more of the Working Ahead suggestions before the next session. If time remains in this session, invite participants to share discoveries from previous Working Ahead activities.

Closing Worship

Tell participants that you would like volunteers to join you in leading the class in a prayer about prayer. Begin by asking for God's strength and guidance in making prayer more important in your own life. Name one or two things you would like your prayers to become (more of a regular habit? more thankful? more informal and spontaneous? more directed to and concerned about people you don't get along with?—you name it) and then pause for participants to add their petitions. Don't be afraid of silence.

After several minutes, wrap up the requests:

Thank You, O Loving Father, for the privilege of prayer. We know that You hear and answer our very thoughts and the words we cannot express. For this, and for the power of Your Holy Spirit we love and praise You. Amen.

Lesson 11

Greetings from the Team (Colossians 4:7–18)

Lesson Aim

Through the example and encouragement of faithful Christians of all times, God provides strength and encouragement for our own lives of faith and our efforts to spread the Good News about Jesus.

Lesson Objectives

By the power of the Holy Spirit working through God's Word, the participants will

1. more clearly understand and appreciate some of the great leaders in the early Christian church;

2. express the encouragement that such Christian leaders can offer to them;

3. seek God's help in demonstrating God's love in their own lives and in their words and actions toward others.

Opening Worship

Begin by reading aloud, or having several volunteers read aloud, the first two chapters in Paul's letter to the Colossians. Then pray stanza 1 of "Let Us Ever Walk with Jesus".

Let us ever walk with Jesus,
Follow His example pure,
Through a world that would deceive us
And to sin our spirits lure.
Onward in His footsteps treading,
Pilgrims here, our home above,
Full of faith and hope and love, Let us do our Father's bidding.
Faithful Lord, with me abide;
I shall follow where You guide.

Approaching This Study

Direct participants to the Study Guide and read the opening three paragraphs, which describe this final portion of Colossians and explain the group project. Divide the class into three groups and assign a section of verses to each group. If your class is very large, you might want to divide it into six groups and assign two groups to each section of verses.

The groups are to read and discuss the assigned verses, look over the Study Guide notes about the people and places named by Paul, and then incorporate their discussion and the notes into a revision of this part of the letter—one that will be meaningful to their classmates.

After all groups have completed their rewriting of the biblical texts, let them read these to the entire class. Encourage questions and discussion from the listeners after each presentation. Group members should respond to any questions on the basis of their study and reading.

Ask the participants to respond to Paul's closing words. What is the purpose of them? What is the tone or feeling they generate? Try to imagine how the Colossian Christians would have responded to the greetings and news.

An Overview

Unit Reading

Ask for a volunteer to read aloud Paul's actual words in **Col. 4:7–18.** How does the original compare with the groups' rewrites?

The Message in Brief

Read this paragraph in the Study Guide aloud.

Working with the Text

Here you may want to divide the class into small groups as in the opening activity and assign each to answer questions regarding the same section of the letter. Then call the groups together for a class discussion. As the groups share their answers, compare these with their earlier descriptions of the people and places.

The Letter Carriers (Colossians 4:7–9)

1. Tychicus and Onesimus were the men Paul charged with delivering his letter to the Colossian Christians. They were apparently with him in Rome at the time Paul wrote. Paul describes Tychicus as "a dear brother, a faithful minister and fellow servant in the Lord." The verses in Timothy and Titus indicate that Tychicus was also an evangelist—someone who accompanied and assisted Paul in spreading the Good News. The words of **Eph. 6:21** echo Paul's description in Colossians.

2. Paul describes Onesimus as "our faithful and dear brother, who is one of you" (a Colossian). It is most likely that he is the runaway slave whom Paul was returning to Philemon. More about him in the final two lessons.

Greetings from Christians (Colossians 4:10-14)

1. Aristarchus had apparently accompanied Paul on earlier missionary travels. It is likely that he, like Paul, was imprisoned for his efforts to spread the Gospel.

2. Paul's description of John Mark indicates that all was forgiven regarding their earlier differences. Paul had been bitterly disappointed with Mark when the young man deserted Paul on his earlier missionary journey. His description of Mark as "a comfort to me," and his request that the Colossians welcome Mark, indicate that Paul practiced the forgiveness that he preached. It also indicates that Mark may have had a change of heart and was now firmly committed to spreading the Gospel and to Paul's person and ministry.

3. Paul describes these men as "the only Jews among my fellow workers for the kingdom of God." From Paul's words, it would seem that they not only helped him tell others about Jesus, they also provided a rich source of personal encouragement and comfort. Let participants reflect on the need for such a two-fold effort among Christians today.

4. It was Epaphras who had started the congregation at Colosse. It was also Epaphras who had brought news of the Colossian Christians to Paul—news that had prompted this letter. Paul describes Epaphras as "one of you" (a Colossian—a Gentile) and a "servant of Christ Jesus . . . [who is] always wrestling in prayer for you." Epaphras was a Christian leader thoroughly committed to caring for those in his charge.

5. Luke was a physician, probably well educated. He was also a close friend of Paul and was well acquainted with the story of Jesus and with the experiences and efforts of the early church. He was the author of the third Gospel and the book of Acts. Let participants explain how this background would make Luke a wonderful listener, comforter, and encourager for Paul in his final days.

The verses in Timothy indicate that Demas left Paul—possibly also the church—to live in Thessalonica.

Greetings to the Christian Community (Colossians 4:15-18)

1. Paul asks the Colossians to read the letter and then to see that it is read by the Laodicean church. The Laodiceans, in turn, are to pass along to the Colossians *their* letter from Paul.

2. Nympha deserved special recognition because she regularly hosted a group of Christians at her house in Laodicea. With this special greeting, Paul not only was personally thanking and encouraging Nympha, he also was drawing the entire church's attention to her unselfish brave deed.

3. Although—as the Study Guide points out—this was customary, doesn't this personal touch add a feeling of warmth and love to the letter? What sort of effect would Paul's "own hand have on the Colossians' attitude toward him and on their reception of his letter and its content?

Review of Colossians

Let participants summarize and elaborate on the five divisions of Colossians: greeting (**1:1–2**); words about the person and work of Christ (**1:3–2:7**); answers to heresy (**2:8–3:4**); encouragement to Christian living (**3:5–4:6**); and personal news and notes (**4:7–18**). If there is time, you might list these divisions on the chalkboard or a sheet of newsprint and ask participants to recall specific points addressed in each.

Applying the Message

On the Larger Scene

You may want to assign the questions to small groups or teams before discussing them with the entire class.

1. Encourage the teams and participants to share their own answers and to question and discuss those of their classmates. Have the changes in our society affected the relevance of Paul's words? Or is Paul dealing with universal issues?

2. Again ask for open discussion of ideas. Participants may want to reflect on Paul's combination of warmth and personal concern coupled with clear, authoritative instruction. How important is it that the communicator be known and respected by readers/listeners? How important is it for a person to know his or her audience?

On a More Personal Level

Allow participants to work through these questions independently. Then let volunteers share their answers with the entire class.

1. You might want to kick off a discussion of this question by explaining your own discoveries and resolutions after studying Colossians. Invite other participants to share their answers.

2. Try to involve the entire class in comparing the church of Paul's time with the church today. There will likely be a fair amount of discussion about whether life was easier for Christians "then" or "now." Try to steer the discussion into an exploration of how Paul's words can most effectively speak to our own church—no matter how the outward trappings have changed through the years. How would *you* feel about living during Paul's day?

Taking the Lesson Home

Encourage participants to complete the Review activity, the Looking Ahead activity, and one or more of the Working Ahead suggestions before the next session. If time remains in this session, invite participants to share discoveries from previous "Working Ahead" activities.

Closing Worship

Read aloud chapters 3 and 4 of Colossians. Then close by praying the final stanza of "Let Us Ever Walk with Jesus".

Let us also live with Jesus.
He has risen from the dead
That to life we may awaken.
Jesus, since You are our head,
We are Your own living members;
Where You live, there we shall be
In Your presence constantly,
Living there with You forever.
Jesus, let me faithful be,
Life eternal grant to me.

Lesson 12

Philemon—Background (Philemon 1–7)

Lesson Aim

God invites and encourages us to pray for one another. Through prayers of thanksgiving as well as ones of petition, we can encourage one another and build stronger bonds with other Christians.

Lesson Objectives

By the power of the Holy Spirit working through God's Word, the participants will

1. more clearly understand the background and motive behind Paul's letter to Philemon;

2. explore and discuss Paul's gracious way of approaching Philemon for a request;

3. describe how Christians can follow Paul's model of thankful prayer in their own prayers for one another;

4. seek God's power and the confidence He gives to expand their own prayers for other Christians.

Opening Worship

Pray stanzas 1–3 of "Lord of All Hopefulness". Then read aloud Paul's letter to Philemon and ask God's blessing on your study.

Lord of all hopefulness, Lord of all joy,
Whose trust, ever child-like, no cares could destroy
Be there at our waking, and give us, we pray,
Your bliss in our hearts, Lord, at the break of the day.

Lord of all eagerness, Lord of all faith,
Whose strong hands were skilled at the plane and the lathe:
Be there at our labors, and give us, we pray,
Your strength in our hearts, Lord, at the noon of the day.

Lord of all kindliness, Lord of all grace,
Your hands swift to welcome, Your arms to embrace:
Be there at our homing, and give us, we pray,
Your love in our hearts, Lord, at the eve of the day.

Approaching This Study

Direct participants to the Study Guide. Ask for several volunteers to read aloud the four paragraphs describing the background to Paul's letter to Philemon. Pause briefly to find out if participants can supply any additional background information about this letter. Then have class members independently read and, on the basis of the brief background information, respond to the four questions in the Study Guide.

Discuss the four questions. Several of the points will become clear as you begin to study Philemon, but for now, solicit the participants' reactions and responses. Question 2 may provoke some debate. It might be helpful to point out that, in the society of his day, Onesimus was the property of Philemon. Slavery was a legal and accepted practice (no matter what we think of it today). Encourage participants to recall these initial reactions as they probe more deeply into the letter itself.

An Overview

Unit Reading

Read aloud **Philemon 1–7**. Then ask participants to compare these verses with Paul's greeting to the Christian church in **Col. 1:1–14**.

The Message in Brief

Read this summary paragraph aloud. Recall your reading of the entire letter during the Opening Worship, and explain that the remainder of Paul's letter consists of his plea on behalf of Onesimus, a closing greeting, and a prayer for grace.

Working with the Text

Either allow participants to complete this section independently, or divide them into groups and let each group discuss and answer the questions. Then discuss the section with the entire class.

Salutation and Greeting (Philemon 1–3)

1. In his letter to the Colossian church, Paul does not refer to himself as "a prisoner of Christ Jesus." Let participants explain how this reminder might stir compassion in Philemon and soften his heart toward Onesimus. It is also important for Philemon to realize that service and devotion to Christ is costly—it cost Paul his freedom; and it will require Philemon the difficult task to forgive and demonstrate a changed attitude.

2. Paul describes Philemon as a dear friend and co-worker.

3. The two references to Archippus indicate that he was deeply involved in the task of spreading the Good News about Jesus. Ask participants to explain why this may have led Paul to refer to Archippus as "our fellow soldier."

4. The Colossian Christians regularly met in Philemon's home. They would certainly see and/or hear about his treatment of Onesimus, and they would be influenced by Philemon's actions and attitudes. In addition, Christians are deeply involved in and concerned about one another. What one Christian does will affect all others. Perhaps Paul wanted to plant this reminder in Philemon's mind as he read the apostle's later request.

Thanks and a Prayer (Philemon 4–7)

1. Paul offers thanks for Philemon's strong faith and for his deeds of love to the other Christians in Colosse.

2. Let participants explain how deeds of love can "refresh" other Christians—can restore flagging spirits and inspire new hope and commitment. Paul prays that God will make Philemon even more active in

sharing his faith and help him more fully realize the blessings that are offered in Christ. How does this request of God relate to what Paul is about to ask Philemon?

3. Let participants speculate on the reaction Paul's words might have generated. It's important to realize that Paul is not just applying the "soft soap" here. All of our actions toward and with other Christians need to be inspired by genuine love for them as people whom Christ loves and empowers. And we need always to build one another up with genuine words of praise and encouragement. Paul approached the problem in a Christian manner. Let participants consider whether this sort of approach to problems or disagreements would be helpful for Christians to use today.

Applying the Message

On the Larger Scene

You may choose either to assign these questions to small groups for discussion or to discuss them with the entire class.

1. Encourage participants to discuss their personal experiences regarding this question. Often when Christians tell other Christians that they will pray, or are praying, for them, it is done in a sorrowful, somber manner, and accompanied by a gentle pat on the shoulder. That is fine—it's even appropriate—since most often these are prayers for people who are experiencing grief or difficulty. But aren't there other situations that should elicit our prayers for others—and our oral affirmations that we are praying for each other in all circumstances including successes, happy events, excitement about what they've done for the church or for someone else? Let class members speculate on why Christians seem reluctant to talk about these happy reasons for prayer. What would be the results of these kinds of prayers and reassurances—for both the person praying and the person who is prayed for?

2. Paul's action indicates his trust in God and his trust in Philemon (as a child of God). Let participants talk about evidence of such trust in Christians today.

3. You might want to refer to the earlier discussion about Paul's opening greeting to Philemon, and the effect this would have on his reception to the apostle's request. How will a genuine love for Christ in the other person affect our approach to her or him during times of disagreement or disputes? What difference will this make in our tone of voice, in the words we choose, in our willingness to listen to the other person?

On a More Personal Level.

Allow time for participants to complete this section independently. Then invite volunteers to share their thoughts with the class.

1. Answers will vary.

2. The great thing about a written word of praise is that we can turn to it again and again—especially during times when we feel discouraged or lonely. Ask participants to suggest general categories of people who might benefit from such notes; the pastor, the pastor's wife or children, friends, parents, children, etc. Encourage them to think of specific names and then to put their thoughts on paper.

Taking the Lesson Home

Encourage participants to complete the Review activity, the Looking Ahead activity, and one or more of the Working Ahead suggestions before the final session. If time remains in this session, invite participants to share discoveries from previous "Working Ahead activities.

Closing Worship

Offer a prayer of thanks to God for specific Christians in your congregation, mentioning contributions they make to the church. You begin the prayer, and then invite volunteers to add names of additional Christians and their contributions to the church. Close the prayer with words of thanks for God's great gift of Jesus, through whom we have the power to love and encourage one another.

Lesson 13

Philemon—The Request (Philemon 8–25)

Lesson Aim

In Christ, we are all equal—equally loved and equally valued. Through Christ, we are capable of expressing love to others, regardless of differences such as race, social class, gender, nationality, or age.

Lesson Objectives

By the power of the Holy Spirit working through God's Word, the participants will

1. see in Paul's letter to Philemon a beautiful example of how Christ's love can effect reconciliation between Christians;

155

2. name ways in which they can, through God's power, use Christian love to effect changes in their own and others' attitudes and behavior;

3. express what they have learned from their study of Paul's letters to the Colossians and Philemon;

4. reflect on the need to focus constantly on Christ and His power in their lives.

Opening Worship

Begin with a group prayer for specific Christians in your class and congregation. This will be similar to the prayer suggested in last session's closing worship. However, this time, you will focus on needs and requests rather than thanksgiving. Invite participants to name specific individuals and their needs. After noting these on the board or a piece of paper, ask class members to bow their heads for prayer. One by one, mention the listed individuals and their needs, and then pause briefly while you and the participants offer silent prayers for them. Conclude the prayer by thanking God for His promise to hear and answer us.

Ask participants quickly to review the situation (Session 12) that prompted Paul's letter to Philemon. Then read the letter to Philemon aloud.

Approaching This Study

Direct participants to the Study Guide material for this final session. Work through this opening section with the entire class. Have a volunteer read the information in the first three paragraphs, then discuss the questions. Rather than comment on participants' answers to the first question, explain that the lesson material deals with this very issue.

In the passages from **1 Corinthians** and **Galatians**, Paul advocates equality among all Christians, regardless of nationality, race, or social status. Such an idea would certainly have caused a stir among the people of his day.

An Overview

Unit Reading

Ask a volunteer to read this final section of Philemon. Let participants point out how Paul maintains a warm, intimate tone throughout the letter.

The Message in Brief

Read this summary paragraph aloud and invite questions or comments from the class.

Working with the Text

Either allow participants to complete this section independently, or else divide them into groups and let each group talk about and answer the questions. Then discuss the section with the entire class.

The Request (Philemon 8–14)

1. Paul's position of authority as Philemon's spiritual leader, and the Gospel message of forgiveness in Christ, entitle him to demand that Philemon show love and forgiveness to Onesimus. Encourage participants to discuss the effectiveness of this method as compared with Paul's loving encouragement. How is Paul's approach a model for all Christians, especially those who are in authority? Paul identifies the motive for demonstrating love and forgiveness as Jesus' love.

2. Onesimus became a Christian, probably through his contact with Paul. Because of this conversion, Paul could call Onesimus his spiritual "son."

3. Ask participants to explain the difference in Onesimus' relationship with Philemon now that the slave had become a Christian. How is he now truly useful to Philemon? In what double sense—spiritual and physical—can Onesimus be far more effective in the household of Philemon?

4. Paul's writing is peppered with phrases such as "an old man and now also a prisoner of Christ Jesus," "my son Onesimus," "useful . . . to me," "him—who is my very heart," "I would have liked to keep him with me."

As Christians we have an obligation to look out for one another, to be sensitive to the needs and feelings of one another. If Philemon's behavior toward Onesimus will affect Paul and—just as important—the spreading of the Gospel, isn't Paul right to say so?

Motivation for Philemon (Philemon 15–20)

1. Paul is indirectly suggesting that God may have been working something good out of the incident with Onesimus. Ask participants, "In what larger sense (larger than the individual reconciliation between Philemon and Onesimus) can good come from Philemon's experiences?" How might a change in Philemon's attitude affect his dealings with the other slaves? How might the incident affect other Christians' attitudes?

Now that Onesimus had become a Christian, the relationship between him and Philemon was one of spiritual brothers—regardless of their status as master and slave. How will the spiritual relationship affect interactions between these men?

2. The hand-written promise to repay Philemon would certainly add weight and reassurance to Paul's words. It also reflects Paul's deep personal involvement in the whole matter.

3. In what sense does Philemon owe Paul his "very self"? Remember that it was through Paul's work that Philemon became a Christian. How is Philemon's debt really owed to God—through Paul? Also let the class consider our obligations to fellow Christians. How does that fact that we are united-one-in Christ affect our relationship with one another? Our concern for each other? Our acts of generosity and love toward one another?

4. Philemon's acts of love toward other Christians gave them new, "fresh hope and commitment. Think of how Paul would be "refreshed" by seeing Philemon and Onesimus reconciled and made brothers in Christ. Let participants reflect on how much such a thing would mean to this apostle who was confined to Roman imprisonment. Why do Christian leaders often need "refreshing" even more than the rest of us? Encourage the class to suggest ways in which we can provide such renewal and restoration to our leaders.

A Confident Greeting (Philemon 21–25)

Paul's confidence in Philemon is demonstrated by the manner in which he approaches him with this request and by the fact that Onesimus accompanied the request. Paul's confidence in God is even more clearly demonstrated by those same acts, since Paul trusts that God will bring about a change in Philemon and reconciliation between slave and master. Paul's confidence in prayer is evident throughout this and all his letters. He speaks of it frequently. He talks of the results of prayer as if he expects them-even as if they had already happened. And in **verse 22** Paul speaks of the "guest room" that must be ready after prayers for his freedom are answered.

Applying the Message

On the Larger Scene

Since there is only one question in this section, you may want to assign it to small groups for discussion and response before talking about it with the entire class. Then let a person from each group report his or her answers to the entire class. Groups should note that, while laws may be good and necessary for the sake of justice (people are sinful, and some will do "the right thing" only when forced to do so), laws do not change attitudes. Only love can do this. Let participants talk about how Christians might help to change attitudes as they share Christian love. This is no small task; it's much easier to use force. Can we learn anything about techniques of "applying love" from Paul's letter to Philemon?

Do participants have a clearer understanding of why Paul didn't insist that Philemon free Onesimus (the introductory question)? How about the previous session's question about why Paul's letter to Philemon is included in our Bible?

158

On a More Personal Level

You might want to discuss these with the entire class, since they offer a good opportunity for reviewing the course.

1. Both letters make frequent mention of Christ, a "full understanding of Christ," and the power for new life and change that Christ offers. Paul urged all these Christians to look again at Christ, at His power and love. They needed to take a fresh hold on—a new look at—Christ—His complete supremacy and total sufficiency.

2. Let participants explain why we need to clarify and to revise constantly our own look at Christ. Our confirmation image of Christ may not suffice for adult problems. Our growth in faith requires continual searching—with the help and guidance of God's Spirit—to see more clearly and understand Christ and His guidance in our lives.

3. As you discuss participants' insights and feelings about Paul, help them consider how his qualities as a Christian leader were tempered and enriched by his very human characteristics-both the good and the bad. In his letters, Paul can at times seem petty, whiny, and even self-centered. But he knows this about himself and doesn't hesitate to point out his flaws. It is exactly these weaknesses that heighten the apostle's awareness of Christ's grace, power, and sufficiency in his life. Because he is weak, he understands weakness in others. Because he knows his flaws, he under- stands what humility and grace are all about.

Is Paul someone that participants would like to know personally? Why?

If any class members have kept a notebook on Paul, encourage them to share their discoveries and thoughts as part of this discussion.

Taking the Lesson Home

Even though this is the final session of the course, you might encourage participants to complete the Review activity, the Looking Ahead activity, and the Working Ahead suggestions as review and application of the material studied.

Closing Worship

As a concluding prayer for the course, read the beautiful words of thanks to Christ in stanzas 1 and 2 of "In You Is Gladness." Then close with Paul's final words to Philemon: "The grace of the Lord Jesus Christ be with your spirit."

In You is gladness
Amid all sadness,
Jesus, sunshine of my heart.
By You are given
The gifts of heaven,
You the true Redeemer are.
Our souls are waking;
Our bonds are breaking,
Who trusts You surely
Has built securely
And stands forever. Alleluia!
Our hearts are pining
To see Your shining,
Dying or living,
To You are cleaving;
Now and forever. Alleluia!

If He is ours,
We fear no powers,
Not of earth or sin or death.
He sees and blesses
In worst distresses;
He can change them with a breath.
Wherefore the story
Tell of His glory
With hearts and voices;
All heav'n rejoices
In Him forever. Alleluia!
We shout for gladness,
Win over sadness,
Love Him and praise Him
And still shall raise Him
Glad hymns forever. Alleluia!

CPSIA information can be obtained
at www.ICGtesting.com
Printed in the USA
FSOW02n1055200915
11316FS